The Overnight City

*The Life and Times of Van Lear,
Kentucky, 1908-1947*

The Overnight City

The Life and Times of Van Lear,
Kentucky, 1908-1947

Clyde Roy Pack

storyatom™

Franklin, Tennessee

To Wilma Jean, my very own coal miner's daughter.

Other books by Clyde Roy Pack

The Best of Poison Oak

Muddy Branch: Memories of an Eastern Kentucky Coal Camp

Coal-Camp Chronicles

Dear Hearts and Gentle People

Going Back

Pretty Babies Grow Up Ugly (with Todd Pack)

"But it is by newspapers that we chronicle the sojourn of mankind here upon earth. Why, with your name in the paper, it is quite possible that someone one hundred years or more from now will read your name and, for the moment, you are alive again, if only in the mind of the reader."

William W. Johnstone

Contents

Introduction

C oal was discovered in the future Commonwealth of Kentucky by the explorer Dr. Thomas Walker on a spring day in 1750.

Walker was co-founder of a Virginia concern called the Loyal Land Company, which had received a grant of 800,000 acres in what is now southeastern Kentucky. During an expedition to find a good place to build a settlement, he noted that he had found "some small pieces of coal." He soon found more. He found so much, in fact, that he began referring to the area simply as "Coal Land."

Coal was a valuable resource for Kentucky's early settlers, fueling their stoves and blacksmith fires as well as giving them a commodity to trade for much-needed supplies. Commercial mining, however, didn't begin until 1820 in western Kentucky, where coal dug near the Muhlenberg County community of Paradise could be shipped down the Green River to larger towns such as Owensboro and Evansville, Indiana. Eastern Kentucky's expansive coal seams were deemed too remote for commercial mining operations until the arrival of the railroads around the turn of the century.

One of the region's best-known coal towns was built in a part of Johnson County previously known as Millers Creek, about five miles southwest of the county seat of Paintsville. Plans to develop Millers Creek were first outlined in the local weekly, *The Paintsville Herald*:

> **February 27, 1908**—The Millers Creek coal field, not yet developed, is great and will produce a very high grade, equaling the Muddy Branch product. The Millers Creek field will soon be operated by a company with a great financial backing, and will, it is said, have the largest and best plants installed of any mining section in Kentucky. C. W. Watson, the Baltimore multi-millionaire is at the head of the company that will operate in the Millers Creek field. A branch railroad is to be constructed to this field.

That article signaled the beginning of what was to become one of the better-known coal towns in eastern Kentucky, or perhaps even the world, thanks to country music star Loretta Lynn, who was born there in 1932. In 1969, she released "Coal Miner's Daughter," which included the line, "My daddy worked all night in the Van Lear coal mines...." *Coal Miner's Daughter* was also the name of Lynn's 1976 autobiography, which was made into a 1980 movie that was nominated for seven Academy Awards, including Best Picture. In 1986, the Pike County-born country singer Dwight Yoakam painted a less sentimental portrait of coal-camp life in "Miner's Prayer," a song on his debut album, *Guitars,*

Cadillacs, Etc., Etc.: "I still grieve for my poor brother, and I still hear my dear old mother cry / Late that night, they came and told her he'd lost his life down in the Van Lear mines."

Van Lear was dubbed by one newspaperman early on as "the overnight city" because it sprang so quickly from the mostly unoccupied farmland five miles southwest of Paintsville, the county seat of Johnson County.

It was named for Van Lear Black, a director of the Consolidation Coal Company—Consol, for short—which acquired the rights to land along Millers Creek from the Northern Coal and Coke Company. There is no record that Black, a civil aviation pioneer and chairman of *The Baltimore Sun* newspaper from 1914 until his death in 1930, ever set foot in Johnson County, but, in 2008, his grandson, Van Lear Black III, and his great grandson, Van Lear Black IV, served as grand marshals of the town's annual celebration.

Van Lear, Kentucky, was incorporated in 1912 and Consol mined coal there, at one time operating five mines, 24 hours a day. In 1945, Consol merged with Pittsburgh Coal Company. It then divested itself of the Millers Creek property.

The following article in the paper leaves little doubt as to how this tiny town, nestled neatly among the foothills of Appalachia, and Consol, teamed to prosper and play such an important role in coal production in eastern Kentucky over the next four decades:

March 18, 1915—There is a great business and commercial awakening throughout the Big Sandy coal fields, comprising mainly the region of the Levisa Fork and its tributaries, the counties of Johnson, Floyd and Pike. The upper Big Sandy Valley was penetrated several years ago by the Chesapeake & Ohio Railroad, but only in recent years have coal developments reached their activity. During the past two years, numerous short line branches have extended out into extensive coal beds as well as almost untouched forests, while along the old line new cities and new coal and lumber enterprises have sprung into existence, established towns, county seats, etc., have also increased wonderfully along all lines of commercial importance.

First, perhaps, in importance of the new cities that have grown is Jenkins, with a rapidly increasing population of between 4,000 and 5,000 people, the seat of the extensive coal and industrial development work of the Consolidation Coal Company at the headwaters of Elkhorn Creek, a tributary of the Big Sandy, immediately beyond the Pike County line in Letcher County, reached by the Sandy Valley & Elkhorn, owned by the Baltimore & Ohio. Less than three years ago when the first tree was felled on Elkhorn Creek, where now stands the city of Jenkins, that section was practically a forest, with only an occasional farmhouse, where moonshining, marauding and murder flourished.

Promoters of the city came and set themselves to work against what seemed to be impregnable barriers. They were 30 miles from a railroad line and twice as far from a telegraph office, with almost impassable roads. It was a gigantic task, but John G. Smyth, a prince of sturdy, resolute manhood, came and blazed the trail and helped to lay the foundation for one of the biggest development

14

enterprises in the South. Smyth was manager of the Elkhorn division of the company. He had gained a wide experience in the West Virginia and Pennsylvania fields, where he was prominently identified with the operations of the Consolidation Coal Company, and was chosen to superintend and manage the new territory

Pikeville, the county seat of Pike County, is an old town, and previous to a few years ago was of little consequence except as a shipping point for a large territory in Eastern Kentucky, being at the head of navigation of the Big Sandy. Four or five years ago there was a better spirit manifest and Pikeville began to grow. The same spirit that imbued the rapidly developing industrial South made its impress on Pikeville. The men behind the push knew there were abundant resources surrounding the town—virgin fields of practically all kinds of hardwood and mountains of coal. Pikeville has good banking institutions, all in a sound, healthy condition, ably and prudently managed. Pikeville's banking institutions, so far, have been one of the most potent agencies in building up the trade and industries of the picturesque little city. In educational facilities, Pikeville is thoroughly abreast of the times. The public schools are provided in adequate numbers with a competent number of instructors, and there is also located here one of the best colleges in the state, this is the Pikeville Collegiate Institute, in which hundreds of students are enrolled annually.

Prestonsburg and Paintsville are both thriving, growing cities of the present day, the former in Floyd County and the latter in Johnson County, both on the main line of the Big Sandy branch of the Chesapeake & Ohio Railroad. Prestonsburg has numerous coal lines and tracts of extensive hardwood fields surrounding in close proximity. The Elkhorn Fuel Company, a gigantic coal operation at Wayland, on Beaver Creek, not far from Prestonsburg, is employing an army of men. Prestonsburg has for years been an important residence city, but with the vast development surrounding today is a business center of note, a large number of business blocks having been built during the past two years.

Paintsville, the home of the late John C. C. Mayo, is in a splendid agricultural region, while coal and timber fields abound. Three miles above Paintsville is Van Lear, an "overnight" city of the Consolidation Coal Company, where it has an extensive operation, second to its Jenkins and McRoberts plants.

Just seven years after an interest in the Millers Creek coal seam was made public, the town of Van Lear was affecting the entire Big Sandy Valley.

April 1, 1915—Van Lear electric power is now being wired to Prestonsburg for the lighting of the town and power. This is the beginning of the work that is to connect all the towns of the Sandy Valley by the same electric system. From Jenkins to Van Lear the electric power will be joined together, supplying Paintsville, Van Lear, Pikeville, Prestonsburg, Jenkins and all other points and coal mines along the line. By this arrangement all the business will be under one head and a much better service will be furnished all towns. Heretofore, only a night current has been supplied to Prestonsburg and Pikeville but now both day and night service will be rendered all towns.

The object of these lines being connected is to insure a better system. When the Van Lear plant happens to be down by accident, power will come from Jenkins and the consumer will not be inconvenienced.

Best of all, however, comes the good news that a reduction is to be made in the rates for electricity. This is not only good news but justice to the consumers. The rate has been too high all the time and now a reduction is gladly welcomed even at this late hour.

The first draft of Van Lear's history was recorded in the pages *The Paintsville Herald.* In the 39 years covered in this book—from the initial reports on the Millers Creek project to the sale of the town by Consolidation Coal Company—more than 130 articles were printed, including more than 15 stories of mining fatalities, along with eight killings, two suicides, and two military deaths.

The stories are presented in chronological order, in order to give readers a sense of the flow of everyday life in the community. As you read these articles, please remember they are reprinted as they originally appeared in the pages of *The Paintsville Herald*, many decades ago. It was common for editors at the time to use racial and ethnic slurs we find offensive today. I opted not to omit them, however, because they convey the attitudes and social norms of the time.

I wish to thank the staff of the Johnson County Public Library as well as the volunteers at the Van Lear Historical Society for their help in researching the story of Van Lear. I am also grateful to the anonymous correspondents who recorded the town's history and to

Paula Halm, the current editor and publisher of the *Herald*, for allowing me to include many of those reports in this book.

Clyde Roy Pack
July 2014

Chapter One: 1914-1919

*A*s important as Consol was in the development of the town of Van Lear, and as interesting as the story of Van Lear Black might be, this book is much more than a story of the company or any one man. What we've done is develop through research a chronological history of the people who lived there, as documented in the pages of The Paintsville Herald.

Of course, there were also articles dedicated to the company itself, and we have included them wherever and whenever they occurred. But by and large, realizing it was the people who lived there that made the town what it became, more often than not, the items we found in those brittle, yellowed pages were dedicated to the people who resided in this little "overnight city."

At least one killing made the paper during the teen years, as did the capture of a couple of bootleggers. And in 1917, a measles epidemic closed the Van Lear schools.

The hiring of teachers made news and someone in the community took on the responsibility of reporting the social news, informing the public about who was visiting whom, who made trips to town, and who had been visited by the stork.

The big story, however, was President Woodrow Wilson's enacting the Selective Service Act of 1917, and the listing of Van Lear men who were among the first 300 from Johnson County who were called for examination.

July 9, 1914—News reached here Saturday from Van Lear notifying the authorities of a shooting scrape that had just occurred at that place. Sheriff Geo. W. Spears left immediately for the scene of the shooting and on arriving at Van Lear learned that Jake Clark, formerly of Floyd County, but who now resided in Van Lear, had shot and fatally wounded a Hungarian miner by the name of Chacowzkor.

The shooting occurred Saturday evening and the unfortunate man expired Sunday night.

It is said that the trouble started over Clark's boy throwing a rock and accidently striking the Hunk's wife on the head. It appears that the boy was out hunting a cow near the Hunk's home, and while throwing at the cow one of the rocks hit the Hunk's wife making a slight scalp wound. It is said the Hunk became enraged over the incident and caught and whipped the youngster. The boy then went to his own home in tears and told his father the Hunk had beat and abused him. Upon hearing his son's story, the father, too, became enraged and told the boy to show him the man that had used him so roughly. They soon found Chacowzkor and the shooting occurred. Two of the balls took effect in the legs while the third and fatal shot took effect in the side, striking a rib and ranging downward through the abdomen perforating the intestines. These are the facts as reported to the Herald.

Clark was arrested by Sheriff Spears and brought to Paintsville and placed in jail. The trial was set for Wednesday but on account of the absence of attorneys Fogg and Kirk, the case was continued until Thursday, July 16.

Clark was refused bond.

It was nearly two years later when law enforcement made the news again.

February 17, 1916—Friday was a lucky day for Town Marshal K. Price. On Friday, February 4, he got word that someone was selling whiskey in Van Lear, so he soon got warrants for the arrest of a young man by the name of Delong. He phoned to Sheriff Spears and they went after Delong and ran him down to the river when he ran up a hollow. Both Sheriff Spears and Marshal Price leveled guns at him and invited him back. Of course he came. The Sheriff took him to Paintsville and turned him over to Jailer Trimble.

On the next Friday, the 11th, Mr. Price got more news of two Negroes who were bootlegging. While Judge Lynch was writing the warrants, the Negroes stepped into the store. The Judge, being always for law and order, assisted Marshal Price in arresting the coons.

They were placed in the lock-up and next morning Mr. Price took them to Paintsville.

The Negroes were slick in the business. They had been here about two weeks. They would put on their mining outfits, go to the mines and then come out, go to the commissary supposedly to buy goods. But K. Price is an old officer and hard to fool. When he gets the right dope, he always gets his man. Judge Dan P. Lynch, as well as Mr. Price, are always for right and are always ready to go out at any time of the night to put down trouble.

It appears that a local reporter was hired (or perhaps volunteered) to keep Herald readers abreast of social activities.

March 2, 1916—Burns Combs, express agent at Van Lear Junction, who has been very sick for the past week, is able to be out again.

Miss Elizabeth Patrick of Salyersville was the guest of Misses Ollie and Lucy Duncan Wednesday.

G. C. Wells passed thru the city Wednesday evening en route to Prestonsburg.

Mrs. S. B. Shell, of West Van Lear, was calling on Mrs. Hager Thursday afternoon.

Elmer Conley and Frank Duncan were visiting friends at Hager Hill Wednesday.

Mrs. E. L. McCue returned Thursday night from Ashland where she has been visiting her parents Mr. and Mrs. Chas. Burk.

Mrs. Press Childers was calling on Mrs. M. L. Watson Wednesday evening.

Mrs. L. Phelps and Miss Ethel Williams went to Paintsville Thursday.

Curt B. Rice, who was calling on Miss Ollie Duncan Saturday and Sunday, left Monday morning for his home in Salyersville.

Mr. and Mrs. Seldon Smith were the Sunday guests of Mr. Smith's parents, Mr. and Mrs. Will Smith.

Misses Arcie and Stella Johnson, of Hager Hill, were calling on Miss Mae Blair Saturday evening.

Ham Witten, of Tom's Creek, was calling on Miss Verlie Johnson Sunday afternoon.

Mrs. J. A. McCaskey and Mrs. R. L. Mays spent Sunday with their father Mr. M. T. Duncan.

Miss Lillie Burton was called to the bedside of her mother who was thrown from a horse a few days ago and was badly injured. She and her little niece, Thelma Chaffin, left at once for her home at Louisa.

Clyde Carter was in our town on business Monday.

The following teachers have been hired to teach at the Van Lear Graded School. Prof. Nathan George, Edna L. Conley, Mearle Riffe, Sola Spears and Elsie Webb.

February 16, 1917—The Van Lear schools were closed Monday on account of an epidemic of measles at Van Lear. Prof. Nathan George, principal of the school and Miss Sola Spears, a teacher, were here Monday.

With World War I raging in Europe, in June 1917, President Woodrow Wilson enacted the draft via the

Selective Service Act of 1917. At first, all men between ages 21 and 31 were called. Later the age limits were changed to men between ages 18 and 45. The act allowed exemptions for dependency, and essential occupations.

August 23, 1917—Thursday, Friday, and Saturday this week the Local Exemption Board will examine the first three hundred men called for service in the United States Army. These men have been called to Paintsville for the last three days of this week. In this first three hundred are many who are unfit for service in the army on account of physical disability, and of course, will be exempted when they are examined.

Most all of the married men are asking exemptions on the grounds of dependents, over two hundred having filed their papers on these grounds. Johnson County must furnish 150 men and if they cannot get them out of the first 300 called, others will be called by the board at once.

Following are the names of men from Van Lear who were among the first three hundred called.

Frank Daniels, Bayless Raymond Litteral, Albert E. Riley, E.C. Fairchilds, Thomas Mullins, Isaac Brown, Charles Adkins, Andy Greathouse, Oscar Fitch, Andy Wells, Finley Jarrell, H. G. Smith, W. R. Fritts, Thomas Watson, Clyde Meddings, Marcus Adams, John Smith, William Hall, J. E. Messer, Ronnie Smith, Frank H. Price, Enoch Pressley, Walton Holmes, Alonzo Carter, George

Savko, Paris Pelphrey, Arch Castle, James C. Layne, Wesley Adams, Albert Wolfe, Menifee Whittaker, William Walter, Wiley W. Price, George Colenoff, Elbert Dye, William Fraley, Elisha Howes, Edmund H. Price, Buford Hall, Ballard Rice, and Thomas Hart.

From time to time, Consol used the newspaper to remind readers how the company, the town, and its people were progressing. Such is the following article.

December 20, 1917—Nothing is more strongly indicative of the advancement of any section along commercial lines than the development of its hidden resources and nothing has contributed in greater measure to build up Johnson County, Paintsville, and the Big Sandy Valley than has the Consolidation Coal Company's operation at Van Lear. From a poor and thinly settled farming section has sprung up the hustling town of Van Lear, with a population of about 2,500, with good schools, good churches and an ideal citizenship.

The company owns about 100,000 acres of coal lands on Millers Creek and is assured of coal for years to come. This company has opened the avenues of commerce to this section in such a manner that its value cannot be overestimated.

Had coal not been discovered in the hills and mountains of this county and men of far sighted business acumen been attracted to our section, this would still be an undeveloped portion of the country. Today, there are thousands of men given regular employment, and are paid the highest wages for their labor of any class of workman. A miner, as a rule, has within his own power to make this time profitable or unprofitable; it is up to him, so to speak, for he is paid by the ton.

Many advantages are given the miners at Van Lear. Good houses, well- constructed, plastered, supplied with electric lights and all conveniences. The houses are fenced off and ample grounds for gardens are supplied and a lively interest is taken by the miners in producing good gardens. In addition to all these conveniences, the company has built and maintains a road at its own expense, a distance of some five miles. This road is free to the public.

Van Lear is located on Millers Creek about four miles from Paintsville on the Millers Creek Railroad, connecting with the main line of the Big Sandy Division of the C & O at Van Lear Junction. The town is a model mining town. It is incorporated with good officials, a moving picture show, billiard and pool room, soda fountain, churches, schools, excellent stores, barber shops, and in fact all conveniences of the larger towns. Everything for the good of the county or the valley is strongly advocated and encouraged by the Consolidation Coal Company. Their first thought is always for the betterment of the conditions of their men, next the up building of the county and valley.

Mr. Garner Fletcher, the popular manager of the Millers Creek Division of the Consolidation Coal Company, is well liked by all his employees. He is a broad-minded man who knows his men and is ever watchful for their interests. In all movements of the good of the county, Mr. Fletcher and his loyal employees are found ready and willing to do more than their part. In the Red Cross work, the Army Y. M. C. A. work, the sale of Liberty Bonds, and all other good movements, have been liberally subscribed to at Van Lear. Mr. Fletcher is deeply interested in churches and schools and his efforts along these lines have made Van Lear one of the best mining towns in the state. It is the largest operation on the Big Sandy River and one of the most modern in the country.

The operations of this company at Van Lear, not only helps to increase the business of the merchants of Paintsville, but Johnson, Floyd and Martin counties are greatly benefitted, as a large number of men from these counties are employed. These men spend their money to a large extent with their home merchants. A better market for farm products has been created by this company and anything the farmer has to sell can be disposed of at the mines. The whole valley has benefited by this coal operation.

What this company has done for this section can be estimated by comparisons of the conditions before and after they started their operation. It is one of the first companies to increase the wages of its employees when conditions warrant. No company in all the valley will go farther to assist their employees than will the Consolidation Coal Company at Van Lear, Ky.

Two large stores are located at Van Lear, one at the center of the town, near the post office and main office buildings, known as the main store, while at No. 5 mine, another store is located to make it convenient for those living in that section to be supplied with merchandise, sold to the people at reasonable prices. Ice in the summer, and coal and merchandise all year round are delivered to all mining houses.

As a rule, the miners are thrifty, progressive and saving, many of them banking a large portion of their earnings each month. Schools have been arranged on the creek to make it convenient for the children to get an education. The best of instructors are employed and their school system is second to none in the valley. Churches of most all denominations can be found at Van Lear and those who want to worship in the church of their choice can find church conditions ideal.

All the mines are equipped with the latest mining machinery and every precaution known to modern mining is used to make the mines safe and the surroundings healthy for the men. The latest mine to open is No. 155, better known to those residing as Mine No. 5. This mine being the last one started. It is said to be the most modern mine in all the valley. Experienced mine foremen, superintendents, and skilled workmen can be found at all the mines.

One is at once impressed by the substantial manner in which the operations of this company are put in. Everything about the place is built with an eye to permanency—built to last. The different styles of architecture in the buildings, and the many modern homes make the place look like the model city which it is, more than it does a mining town. Those who have visited Van Lear for the first time have been surprised to see such a modern town on Millers Creek. The good roads and churches, schools and the excellent sanitary condition of things in and around Van Lear, added to all modern conveniences and good wages, have made a happy town indeed for those who are fortunate in living there.

Mr. Fletcher is the general manager and since coming to Johnson County, he has made friends of all who have met him. He has always been ready to help in every way possible to make a bigger and better county. He knows the coal business from start to finish. Associated with him are a number of progressive men who are doing their bit for this section. E. J. Berlin is local auditor; E. R. Price is chief clerk, and John Fuke is chief engineer.

The people of the Big Sandy Valley are proud of the Consolidation Coal Company's operation at Van Lear and point to it with pride.

Then, in little more than a month later, this story was published.

January 26, 1918—The many friends of Mr. Garner Fletcher, who for the past four years has been manager of the Consolidation Coal Company's operation at Van Lear, will regret to know that he has left Johnson County and moved to Jenkins where he has been made manager of that operation. It was a promotion for Mr. Fletcher and one he deserved. Few men have come to Johnson County and made the friends Mr. Fletcher has made in so short a time. The town of Van Lear has been a different town since Mr. Fletcher took charge there. He perfected one of the best working organizations in the state and nothing speaks more for his efficient management than the fact that all this men regret to lose him.

Last Saturday evening these faithful men arranged a banquet for him at the Club House in Van Lear and the many good things these men said about him was conclusive evidence that his work with them was appreciated. A beautiful watch was present to him by these men.

He has been replaced by Mr. E. R. Price. The new manager has been with the company for a number of years and knows every detail of the work. He is well qualified to handle the business of his new post.

Not that it was needed, but the following story serves as ample proof that the town of Van Lear was prospering in the early 1900s.

April 25, 1918—The patriotic citizens of Johnson County and the Big Sandy Valley are proud of the progressive mining town or Van Lear and its patriotic citizens. For the past few weeks, the town has been talking Liberty Bonds and a meeting was held, speeches made, and after placing the matter of Liberty Bonds before the people, they subscribed liberally to the Third Liberty Loan.

All the departments of the Consolidation Coal Company participated in the buying of bonds as the follow table will show: Mine No. 151, $4,700; Mine No.

152, $2,650; Mine No. 133, $5,500; Mine No. 154, $11, 500; Mine No. 155, $7,300; M. C. Ry, $1,700; Store Dept. $950; Aud. Dept., $2,500; P. & M. Dept., $1,650; Con. Dept., $2,300; Eng. Dept., $600; and General, $2,400; for a total of $43,750.. The second Liberty Loan they bought $19,000, and the third Liberty Loan.

In the first Liberty Loan, these patriotic citizens bought $11,000 in bonds. The second Liberty Loan they bought $19,000, and the third Liberty Loan, $43, 750, making total of $73,750 worth of bonds bought in that town.

The Consolidation Coal Company and its employees are doing their part to help win the Great War. The company and its management deserve much credit for their work in the Liberty Loan as well as other movements that help this section and country generally.

Hats off to Van Lear. It can always be depended upon to do the right thing at the right time, and we are indeed fortunate in having this progressive town in our county.

And the residents of Van Lear keep doing what residents do.

May 23, 1918—John McKnight and wife are in Ashland on business.

Lihue Smith of this place is very low with typhoid fever.

Miss Lizzie Mollett of Boons Camp was visiting Miss Pearl Blankenship Saturday night.

The No. 2 store of this place was broken into last week and several articles stolen. The robbers have not been apprehended.

Dr. Lyon and wife and Mrs. Siber, Sam Honaker and wife, and several others from lower Van Lear, attended church here Sunday.

Paris Stambaugh was calling on home folks at Sitka Sunday.

Lincoln Ramey of this place was visiting his father-in-law, Asa Reed on Colvin Branch Saturday and Sunday.

Rev. J. D. Harrington is holding a meeting at this place. All seem to like his services.

Mary Jane Akers of Stambaugh and Sophia Akers of Thealka, are visiting Mrs. Tom Colvin and attending church.

The little son of Mr. and Mrs. Ed Russell, who has diphtheria, is improving.

June 20, 1918—On Friday evening, June 14, the people of Van Lear gathered in the Central Playground to witness the raising of the stars and stripes. Together with the large U. S. flag was the honor flag given Van Lear for her work in the recent Liberty Loan and Red Cross drives, when she went over the top with a vengeance. Quite a crowd was present and enthusiasm ran high.

The program was in charge of Rev. Grumbles of the Baptist Church and every number was appropriate to the occasion and well carried out.

The crowd was assembled around the flag pole by the "Call of the Colors," blown by Fred Hatton, former U.S. soldier-bugler. After this, J. L. Herndon, dressed to represent Uncle Sam, slowly raised the flags as the crowd sang "The Star Spangled Banner." Then followed a salute to the flag and Pledge of Allegiance which was said in unison, everyone joining in heartily. The America's Creed was said in the same way after which Rev. Sturm of the M. E. Church, gave a very able address. The fact that he was vigorously applauded showed truths he uttered, and that they appreciated the things for which the flag stands, and which he was upholding to them. The program closed with the song "America," sang by everyone with a will, and three more rousing cheers were given after which the crowd dispersed.

We do not think the patriotism of Van Lear can be outdone. The people are very proud to have Old Glory floating over them as they go about their daily tasks of helping to win the war, and pledge anew allegiance to our flag, and the Republic for which it stands.

Mr. E. R. Price, manager of the Consolidation Coal Company, gave a speech on the subject, "What Benefit is the Sunday School to the Community." His speech was to the Sunday School Convention held at Van Lear. Many of the leading school workers requested that the Herald publish the speech.

July 11, 1918—"Stevenson once said, 'I think it would be better if we did more practicing and less preaching, for at best I would make a poor preacher,' and I am sure this applies to our relations to the Sunday school for most of us would do better work by closer association with the Sunday school, which reminds me of the strong impression made by General Pershing on his arrival in France illustrating the regard in which the world holds deeds rather than words. When that great commander of the American Expeditionary Forces on his arrival in France gave out the simple but stupendous message of four words, 'Lafayette, we are here,' he won the heart of the French nation as he could not have done by a volume of words, because he demonstrated to that great and heroic people that he is pre-eminently a man not of words, but deeds and I hope through the words here today, great deeds may be accomplished.

"In considering the Sunday school and the community, and in order to properly define the benefits fostered by the Sunday school, it is well to study briefly a standard of community life. By community, we mean society generally—all classes of humanity regardless of station—it is a body of people having common organization with common rights, interests and privileges, living in the same place under the same laws and regulations, but while each member of a community has privileges that are common, our different natures with different motives and desires result in different avocations of life and diversity of accomplishments, but no matter what the nature of human activity, whether it elevates or degrades, whether it is progressive, alert, up and doing, breathing a healthy moral atmosphere, or retrogressive derelict, indifferent, selfish, immoral, it all contributes to the life of the community; the community life is therefore just what we make it, each man, woman, and child forming an integral part and the community life is a mirror reflecting just what we all are; if it is an industrious organization adhering to the religious laws of the Church and the civil laws of our state and country, it has reached a point of efficiency—no matter if village, town, or city, the principle is the same—that breeds happiness, prosperity, and contentment and the community will show it.

"I spoke of a standard or I might say an ideal community life. This does not imply wealth, although when properly applied, wealth can contribute its small share, but the real foundation upon which community life is built is the church which is the bulwark of religious, social, practical and business life, and the Sunday school is the mouthpiece of the church in that it develops the moral character of the individual; it deals with children at the most impressionable age and instills in them the love of scripture; the daily and intensive study of the Bible broadens the mind of youth, endowing it with a knowledge of scripture that will never be forgotten. Too much stress cannot be placed upon the great work of the Sunday school in developing and molding the early life of the individual; it is a place where real and true facts are taught, principles of right and wrong explained which will be employed and proved in daily life, the work of the Sunday school has never been quite so important as today; its opportunity for developing the "man's man and woman" for us in the present crisis as, well as after the war program, is unlimited.

"If patriotism or love or our country is the oil that lubricates the machinery of victory and inspires our men and women to deeds of valor and self-sacrifice, the love of Sunday school will just as surely, through the church, develop character that will defeat the undermining influence that operates against the ideal community life, and as the turbine is the force that generates electricity whose influence is felt in a great many branches of work, so does the influence of the Sunday school spread, reaching out through the church and through the individuals to the community where it inspires obedience to laws, creates industry and makes for the welfare and happiness of all. What I have said applies to the adult as well as to the youth, the same good can be accomplished by the Sunday school in dealing with old and young alike, for the present organized Sunday school grades its work and adopts itself to the teaching of both; in fact, the strongest and most influential Sunday school is the one supported by the men and women where the Adult Bible classes are pillars of the church.

"The Sunday school, my friends, is the last line of defense counting from the enemy back; it is the first line counting in the other direction. Directly back of the Sunday school lies the whole future of the race. There is therefore, no work as important in these days as training the man, woman and child and we can win the war in France and lose it in America if we neglect to prepare the on-coming generation for the victory we shall bequeath it. The past war days will require a spiritual and intellectual development in all communities, among all people, which can be best achieved through the Sunday school.

"In conclusion, the Sunday school educates, it teaches organization, industry, discipline and obedience, all of which are reflected in the life of the community, and great organizations of the Sunday schools in Van Lear among the different churches would be a great benefit to the community and to all others who will support it by word and deed."

Consol was also instrumental in influencing the community to appreciate the arts, as the following item demonstrates.

October 8, 1918—The Consolidation Coal Company at Van Lear, Kentucky, is offering this year a Lyceum Course for the benefit of its people in this community. The full series consists of above attractions (The Bells, The Saxonians, and The Liliuokalani Hawaiians), which will appear at the dates mentioned.

The Coit-Alber Bureau is recommended as having booked the finest talent in the country.

The regular price will be 50 cents for adults and 25 cents for children. For the benefit of those who desire to attend each performance, a season ticket will be sold at the following reduced prices, which will admit to all attractions: Adults $1.50, Children 75 cents.

Advertising matter will be displayed several days prior to each attraction. Season tickets will be on sale at the Van Lear Store, Mine 155 Store, and Office Script Window. Script will be accepted in the purchase of the tickets. This course is something new, and whether or not it well be booked each year, will depend upon the patronage of the people in the community.

And community life continued for the citizens of Van Lear.

January 14, 1919—Ed Cecil, mine foreman at No. 4, had the flu.

Harbor Nickols is recovering from a severe attack of the flu.

Mrs. Lydia Bilby of Matewan, W. Va., is visiting her parents, Mr. and Mrs. Mitchell Short.

Welby Hobgood is convalescing after a very severe attack of flu.

Miss Hattie Morrison has returned after spending the holidays with home folks at Ashland.

Lorenza Poole has been discharged and has returned from overseas duty.

Everett Brown has returned from the army looking fine.

We are glad to note that R. M. Taylor, who was hurt in the mines last week, is able to be out again.

M. L. Price is very sick with flu.

Mrs. J. H. Hereford was a business visitor at Paintsville Monday.

Flem Stambaugh and daughter Gertrude left Monday for an extended visit with relatives at Ashland.

The boiler in the school house burst and the teachers are compelled to teach in the Baptist and Methodist churches.

L. S. Hereford is home on a furlough from Camp Sheridan, Ala. Mr. Hereford is a bright and promising young man and a great favorite with the people at this place. We hope he will soon be home to stay.

Miss Maude Nickols is just recovering from a severe attack of tonsillitis.

Mrs. H. Holbrook was in Paintsville Monday where she had her daughter Maggie's eyes tested and fitted for glasses.

Mrs. Taylor and Mrs. Ealey were shopping in Paintsville Monday.

The many friends of Mr. and Mrs. Jesse Fairchilds will be glad to know they are all able to be up and out after a serious attack of the flu.

Miss Boyd, nurse at this place, is certainly proving herself a friend in need.

Chapter Two: 1920-1929

*T*he twenties, like every place else across the country, roared into Van Lear. Unfortunately, we discovered the first report of a mining fatality at the Consolidation Coal Company. We also read of a serious incident where a train/automobile accident claimed one victim. The decade also featured news items about robbers and moonshiners.

But good news seemed to dominate the 1920s in Van Lear as stories of baseball games, school plays, the honor roll and a new preacher moving to town graced the Herald's pages. We also found stories about Kentucky governor William J. Fields, and the newly elected president of Consolidation Coal Company, visiting the community.

During this time period, The Paintsville Herald printed stories about the Van Lear Boy Scouts, the Rotary Club's efforts to get paved roads for the town, special accolades for a Van Lear serviceman, and about the election of a Van Lear man to a Johnson County office.

By the end of the 1920s, Van Lear had established itself as a genuine, self-sufficient Kentucky city. It even had its own baseball team.

April 12, 1923—Much interest is being shown in the baseball team for Van Lear this year. Frank Price, the manager, is working hard to have one of the best teams on the river. New suits and other equipment have been ordered and the club is selling two automobiles to help pay the expense of getting a real live club in the field.

Society news was reported on a regular basis, usually by a resident in the community. That practice has been carried forward until present day. At one time, The Paintsville Herald *had more than a dozen community correspondents.*

May 24, 1923—The Van Lear School gave four successful plays last week. The first was "The Magic Path," given by the second, third and fourth grades, under the direction of Misses Adcock, Dodson and Barnett.

Tuesday night's play was "The Polly Williams Club," given by the sixth grade under the direction of Miss Norine Barnett. Wednesday night's play was "The Matrimonial Bureau," given by the seventh and eighth grades under the direction of Miss Mattie Duke. The final play was given by the high school under the direction of Miss Margaret A. Motter. The name of the play was "Hiawatha," and was a great success as shown by the loud applause which followed the play.

Edgar Hewlett spent Sunday with Miss Delpha Young.

McKinley Sparks was in Van Lear Monday.

M. K. Harris, of Winifred, is back again.

Mr. and Mrs. Tom Young, Bessie Harris, Edgar Hewlett and Delpha Young were visiting Mrs. Young's sister at Thealka last week.

Mr. and Mrs. J. R. Worland and Miss Dora Salyer spent Sunday evening at Corwin Worland's.

Miss Allie Rice, of Prestonsburg, was visiting Ruth Dickerson.

Mrs. Hattie Young and son Herbert were shopping in Paintsville last week.

Mr. and Mrs. Finley Jarrell were the Sunday guests of Mr. and Mrs. E. F. Harris.

The Ladies Aid of the M. E. Church gave a bazaar Saturday night for the benefit of the church.

Measles are very bad at this place.

Loretta Hager spent Sunday with Miss Birdie Powell.

Miss Bess Powell of Harrisburg, Pa., will spend most of the summer with her niece, Mrs. Jim Cook.

Paintsville and Van Lear had a fine ball game Sunday in favor of Van Lear.

Miss Bertha Spears was operated on for appendicitis.

Estill Daniel, Alex Farmer and Reece Watkins and Miss Ruth Dickerson were the Sunday visitors of Miss Ethel Martin.

Matelin Davis and Mary Castle were visiting at Paintsville Saturday.

Gussie Webb was the Sunday dinner guest of Mr. and Mrs. Charlie Castle.

Jason Hall of Winifred was in Van Lear last week.

Back to baseball.

June 7, 1923—The baseball season has opened at Van Lear and many games have been booked for the season. Last Sunday afternoon a team from Ironton, Ohio, played at Van Lear and it was a poor exhibition of the national sport. The Ironton team was so much outclassed by the fast Van Lear team that it was not the least bit interesting. Van Lear knocked the ball all over the field, making a number of home runs. The Ironton team did manage to score one run while Van Lear piled up 21. It was a poor game.

Next Sunday, the Jenkins team is coming to Van Lear and there will be an entirely different story to relate after the game. Jenkins has a fast team and will bring their "rooters" along to make things lively. Those who attend this game are going to see a real game of baseball.

Dick Howes played second base for Van Lear Sunday and played a good game.

Eventually, Consolidation Coal and the C & O Railroad joined forces to take over the B & O Railroad.

July 5, 1923—The Baltimore and Ohio Railroad Company has sold to the Consolidation Coal Company the Sandy Valley & Elkhorn and Millers Creek railroads, and to the Chesapeake & Ohio railroad the Long Fork railway.

These roads all connect with the Chesapeake & Ohio's Sandy Valley branch and are known as top lines and have been separately operated. The amount involved in the transactions is approximately $8,000,000, the company's announcement stated.

The Sandy Valley and Elkhorn railroad runs from Shelby, Pike County, to Jenkins, Letcher County, and a distance of 31 miles. The Millers Creek line is four miles long and runs from Van Lear Junction, near Paintsville, to Van Lear, seat of the Consolidation Company's mines in Johnson County. The long Fork railway forms the connection between Martin and Weeksbury, Floyd County, on the left fork of Beaver Creek, a distance of 25.5 miles.

Church-related events were often reported in the paper.

September 20, 1923—We have the pleasure of introducing to the people of this section this week, the Rev. Perry H. Hood, a West Virginian, who has been appointed pastor of the M. E. Church, South, at Van Lear. He has already arrived and taken charge of the work and preached to his flock. He was in Paintsville Monday and left in the afternoon for West Virginia where he goes to get Mrs. Hood and four little Hoods who will be with him at Van Lear.

Already we are informed that he is making a hit with the people at Van Lear. Reports from West Virginia say he is a hustler in church work and a valuable citizen for any community.

A cordial invitation is extended you to visit the Rev. Hood at Van Lear at any time. He wants you to hear him preach, visit him at his home, in fact, he wants to be one of us and is here to do all the good he can. We are glad to have him in the county

It seems the Van Lear baseball team soundly defeated a team from Paintsville. In the following news item, the sports reporter was apparently more interested in making excuses for the loss for the home team than in reporting the story of the game.

September 4, 1924—The Paintsville ball team received an overwhelming defeat from the hands of the fast Van Lear nine at Riverside Park last Sunday afternoon. The final score was 12 to nothing in favor of the visiting team. Jasper, the veteran pitcher of the Van Lear club was not wholly responsible for the defeat of the local boys, but it was largely due to excellent fielding of the others.

Ward, who is the strong holder of the mound, was being saved for the game to be played Labor Day and was not in the box, but Hurley held down the mound. At the end of the fourth inning Hurley had let the visiting outfit take nine scores and Pugh was put in in his place, but the game was too far gone for a rally and Van Lear took three runs from Pugh.

This is the worst defeat the Paintsville nine has suffered this year. It was largely due to the fact that the boys were not in form. The same team had defeated Van Lear in a previous game.

And life goes on within the Van Lear community.

September 4, 1924—Ora Gross and Ida Hager were united in marriage last week.

Mr. and Mrs. J. A. Cook are spending their vacation this week.

Mrs. J. R. Worland is improving rapidly.

Tera Cordial has returned after a brief visit with relatives at Winifred.

Mr. and Mrs. Tom Young, and children, were visiting at Lowmansville Sunday.

Mr. and Mrs. Jack Goble have returned from a visit with friends and relatives in Ohio.

Samuel Metzger is the guest of his grandmother Mrs. Fannie Atkinson of this place.

Mr. and Mrs. J. R. Worland were visiting friends in Paintsville Sunday.

Jake Webb left Saturday for W. Va.

Pearlie Harris of Winifred is guest of relatives here.

Miss Mary Conley was visiting Zella Fairchilds Sunday afternoon.

Richard Castle has returned after a brief visit at Portsmouth, Ohio.

Jarvie Sparks was a business visitor here Friday.

Mate Davis left last week for Hardy, Ky.

Steve Lemaster of Winifred was here on business last week.

Mr. and Mrs. John Carroll were the guests of Mr. and Mrs. Freelin Daniel Sunday.

Mr. and Mrs. Olma Sparks and Mrs. Jake Webb and Richard Castle were visiting in Paintsville Sunday.

Darwin Sparks spent Sunday in Paintsville.

A large crowd from here spent Labor Day in Paintsville.

Clara Shaw, teacher at the Van Lear school, submitted her honor roll to the Herald.

November 27, 1924—Grade 8: Eugene Auxier, Ruby Kennard, Edward Lewis, William Kelley and Martha Bass. Grade 7: Special honor: Clarence Wollum, Minerva Burkett, Ada Fields and Evelyn Auxier. Honor: Russell Wollum, Emory Lyon, Gladys Phillips, Louis Blinn and Otchel Daniel.

Sadly, tragic news also had to be reported. The efforts of the reporter to be sensitive to both the family of the deceased and the readers appear obvious.

October 9, 1924—The death angel visited the home of Mr. And Mrs. Frank Davis and took from them their baby. The parents have the sympathy of the community.

Mr. and Mrs. Howard Paynter are the proud parents of a baby girl.

Mr. and Mrs. M. W. Harris were visiting their son Charley and daughter Mrs. W. M. Sparks over the weekend.

Miss Tera Cordial spent the weekend with relatives at White House.

Mr. and Mrs. Erwin Gipson, Mr. and Mrs. Jake Webb were visiting Mr. and Mrs. Proctor Webb Monday evening.

Mr. and Mrs. C. T. Worland, Mrs. Charley Salyer were visiting Mrs. J. R. Worland Sunday.

Belle Hewlett is on the sick list.

Joe Williamson, superintendent of construction work, was in Paintsville Friday on business.

Mrs. E. F. Harris was visiting Mrs. Olma Sparks Monday.

Mrs. Con Daniel was the dinner guest of Mrs. J. R. Worland Friday.

The stork visited the home of Mr. and Mrs. Troy Salyer last week and left an eight pound girl.

J. R. Worland had the misfortune of having his thumb badly cut.

Richard Castle was in Paintsville last week.

Mrs. Edgar Hewlett was visiting her mother Mrs. Tom Young, Friday.

The news came as quite a shock to the friends and relatives of Cam Vanhoose of his unexpected death in Washington. He was formerly of this place.

Mrs. Cranston Salyer was visiting Mrs. Troy Salyer Thursday.

Harvey Williams, of Paintsville, made a business trip to Van Lear Friday evening.

Jarvey Sparks was visiting in Van Lear Tuesday.

Willie Lemaster, of Winifred, was here last week on business.

A reporter from Van Lear High School reported the school's activities on a regular basis.

November 5, 1925—The play, "Bashful Mr. Bobbs," was given the second time at the Van Lear Theatre Tuesday night, October 27. The cast of characters was as follows: Katherine Henderson, Wootsie Collins; Frederick Henderson, Russell Woolum; Mrs. Wiggins, Elizabeth Kemper; Obadiah Stump, Ed Congleton; Frances Whittaker, Beaterice Young; Rosalie Otis, Ruth Dickerson; Mr. Robert Bobbs, Robert Pickerell; Marston Bobbs, Arlo Wallace; Jean Graham, Beulah Hammond; Celeste Vanderpool, Evelyn Hammond; and Julie, Minnie Webb. Miss Elizabeth Gifford was the director.

The staff of the "Miscellany" was elected and the officers are as follows: Editor-in-chief, Douglas Auxier; Assistant editor-in-chief, Robert Pickerell; Poems, William Pack; Themes, Ruth Dickerson; Jokes, Elizabeth Kemper; News, William Kelley; Business manager, Clarence Lyon; Assistants, John Pack, Otchel Daniel; Readers and reporters, Dorothy Kazee; freshman class, Georgia Riffe; sophomore class, Ruth Straton; junior class, Beulah Hammond. Faculty advisor, Miss Elizabeth Gifford, A.B.

Miss Elizabeth Gifford of the high school faculty spent the weekend in Dayton, Ohio, on business.

Miss Elizabeth Kemper and Mr. Bill Pack were elected Yell Leaders Wednesday.

The football squad has received its uniforms and will play its first game October 31 at Jenkins.

The girls' basketball team has been organized and hopes to have a series of games this coming winter.

Mr. Ed Congleton, principal, favored the high school with a violin solo, accompanied by Miss Evelyn Hammond Thursday morning.

The P.T.A. was entertained by the students of Van Lear Schools Thursday evening.

Mr. C.V. Snapp, superintendent, and Miss Gussie Webb, attended the football game at Jenkins Saturday.

Miss Virginia Lambert has been unable to attend school for the past few days.

The boys and girls were very sorry to hear of the death of Mr. Edward Blair of West Van Lear.

The Van Lear High School football team played its first game at Jenkins Saturday, October 31. Due to a late start, it has been impossible to schedule games earlier. This was Jenkins' fourth game. The score was 30-0 in favor of Jenkins. Van Lear made their ten yards four times and held Jenkins once. Jenkins made two touchdowns on rushes, two on intercepted passes and one on a fumbled ball near the opponent's goal.

Van Lear played fairly well considering it to be their first game. Jenkins has a fast backfield and had good interference which in a long way makes a good team. They played hard and were out to win, which they did. It was a clean, manly game on the part of both sides.

A terrible accident at the Main Store took the life of a Van Lear teenager.

November 25, 1925—Ocie Conley, age 15, son of Clifford Conley, was injured at the main store of the Consolidation Coal Company last week by the elevator and died from injuries at the Paintsville Hospital Monday night.

The boy was operating the elevator it is said and was caught between the elevator and the first floor, while his feet were hanging over. His leg was broken and his arm was broken in two different places. Physicians say he was internally injured and that those injuries caused his death.

Funeral and burial took place at Van Lear Wednesday. He was a bright boy and his death has caused a lot of sorrow in the family.

Nearly 20 years after Consol began mining the Millers Creek coal fields, business was so good more houses were required to keep up with company growth.

March 25, 1926—The Consolidation Coal Company is building thirty-five new houses at Van Lear. These houses will help to take care of the shortage of houses for the miners at that place. For some time, every house in Van Lear has been occupied and the company has had demands for more.

By and large, Van Lear was not fraught with criminal activity, but occasionally a crime did occur.

April 22, 1926—Robbers entered the C & O station at Van Lear last Thursday night, rolled the company's safe into the yard, broke it open and got away with $25 or $30 in cash and an insurance policy.

The robbery occurred sometime near midnight or the early morning and the thieves gained entrance into the station by prying open one of the windows.

After gaining entrance to the office, they pushed the safe, which was on rollers, into the yard and by use of heavy implements, pried their way into the safe. The thieves then helped themselves to the cash, amounting to about $28 and a life insurance policy belonging to Mr. Bass. Nothing else, either in the station or in the safe, was disturbed by the culprits. So far, no clue has been developed as to the identity of the yeggmen.

"Yeggman" was slang for someone who breaks open safes to steal the contents.

April 22, 1926—The signal "Play Ball," was sounded for the first time this season to the Paintsville High Tigers at Van Lear Saturday when the local school met a team composed of high school players and town players. The final score showed the Tigers were blanked while the Van Lear team scored 4 runs.

The Tigers played very poor ball and simply gave the game to the opponents. Neither side really earned a run in the full nine innings. The Tiger pitcher walked five players while his team mates made 8 errors. Also, ten of the Tigers failed to connect with the sphere and were struck out.

Van Lear played a very good defensive game and made only 2 errors in the full game and these came at a time when the error counted for nothing. The Van Lear pitcher, Webb, gave only 2 walks and struck out 10 of the Tigers.

Paintsville had a chance to score in the opening inning when Chars. Spradlin reached the third sack with no one down. However, the three players who followed were put out by balls to the field.

In the last inning, with a man on third and a man on second with two down, Crit Wells struck the air three times in succession and the game was over. The two chances above mentioned were the best chances the locals had.

The line-up for Van Lear included Lambert, lf; Lyons ,2d; Woollum, 1st; Daniels, ss; Auxier, cf; Burke, c; Wallace, 3rd; and Webb, p.

The Tiger players were Spradlin, Wheeler, Wells, Miller, Meeks, Sublett, Holbrook, Sherman, Hunter, Clark, Williams and Hall.

The Van Lear crowd showed a fine air of sportsmanship and those who made the trip reported a courteous treatment and an extra good time. These two teams clash again in the near future at Riverside Park, the Tigers' playground.

The coal industry was booming in 1926, and Van Lear was right smack in the middle of it.

April 29, 1926—With the coming of more pleasant weather, industrial conditions in the Big Sandy Valley are taking on new life and conditions at this date point to one of the most active years within the history of the valley. Especially is this true of the coal mining industry in Johnson County. Mining operations at White House, Thealka, Van Lear and Auxier are preparing for an unprecedented run during the coming months.

New equipment and better facilities for producing coal on a larger scale is being undertaken by the Northeast Coal Company with operations at White House, Thealka and Auxier and the Consolidation Coal Company of Van Lear.

The Consolidation Coal Company has just completed thirty-five new houses for the accommodation of more miners at their Millers Creek operation and will build sixty-five more in the near future. It is also expected that this company will install a new tipple at Van Lear at once.

The reports of life in the community ranges from a broken leg to rheumatism to a bad case of pneumonia. But life goes on in Van Lear.

May 6, 1926—Ethel Anderson had the misfortune of getting her leg broken while on a hike last Saturday and was taken to the Paintsville Hospital for treatment.

Anna Laura Sparks was the weekend guest of her grandparents, Mr. and Mr. John Sparks of Paintsville.

Mr. and Mrs. Clyde O'Bryan motored to Louisa Saturday and back Sunday.

Mrs. J. R. Worland is very ill with rheumatism.

Jarvy Sparks was visiting friends and relatives here last week.

Julia, little daughter of Mr. and Mrs. Tom Young, is very ill with bronchial pneumonia.

Mrs. E. F. Harris was in Paintsville Monday.

Alma Sparks, Samantha LeMaster and Dessie May of Paintsville were visiting Mrs. Alma Sparks Sunday.

Hattie O'Bryan of Sip, Ky., is the guest of Mr. and Mrs. Roy Fitch.

Mr. and Mrs. Frank Davis were the dinner guests of Mr. and Mrs. Charley Castle Sunday.

Cova Salyer of Sip, Ky., is the guest of her brother at this place.

Milt Harris and Proctor Slone were here on business last week.

Mr. and Mrs. George Worland were in Paintsville Saturday.

Lora Caudill of Flat Gap, is a visitor at this place.

Uncle John Harris, of Winifred, was the guest of friends and relatives here last week.

This story about a miner—and alleged moonshiner— named Wornick Barbrick appeared in the summer.

June 17, 1926—Chief of Police George W. Spears and assistant George Meddings of Van Lear, brought to Paintsville last Friday morning one of the most complete copper stills ever brought to the Johnson County courthouse. The still was of small capacity, not over five gallons, but was complete in every detail for the manufacture of whiskey.

The Van Lear officers were notified about 4 o'clock Friday morning that a still was in operation at the home of Wornick [Barbrick] and upon arrival found the still was still hot, evidently having been in use all night. The officers also reported that a quantity of mash was also found with the still.

Barbrick, who is a miner at Van Lear, is of Polish descent but speaks English, was arrested and brought to Paintsville together with the still and worm. He did not seem to be wrought up over his arrest and did not deny the charge of possessing a still. In a statement to officers, he said he could only make from three pints to two quarts of whisky in five hours on his small outfit and was evidently making whiskey for his own personal use, as no complaints, is it said, had ever been made of his selling whiskey. Practically all foreigners are addicted to the use of intoxicants and officers believe Wornick [Barbrick] was making whisky only for himself and family.

Barbrick, when tried before Judge Butcher Friday, did not deny the charge of possessing a still. He told the judge he never sold whisky or did anyone any harm but was making whisky for his own use. Under the law Judge Butcher was compelled to hold him to the action of the grand jury in July.

In September 1926, what was recorded as the largest crowd in the history of the town gathered in Van Lear for a big picnic and celebration.

September 8, 1926—Saturday, September 4, is a day long to be remembered by the employees of the Consolidation Coal Company at Van Lear as well as by hundreds of other citizens who spent the day as guests of the company.

The big day started off about 9 o'clock when the program began. Boxing, wrestling, pulling, running, dancing and other contests were decided. At 11:30 the big barbecue was served all present. It consisted of meats and other things to eat and drink. There was more than enough for everybody and to spare.

At noon, the aeroplane was dong stunts in the air for the entertainment of the large crowd. No one has attempted to even guess as to how many were there but the crowd was the largest gathering in the history of Van Lear. People from all sections of the county were there and they were all made to feel perfectly welcome.

In the afternoon, the local baseball club played the crack West Virginia team and won. On Sunday, the same teams played again and the visitors won this game.

A dance platform was built and music for the occasion afforded much pleasure. A band from Ashland furnished the music all day and at night. The picture show was free in the evening and the dance was continued until a late hour.

Everything was free at Van Lear for this day. The company paid the expenses and the manger was there to see that everybody was well taken care of.

This picnic and celebration on the part of the company was greatly appreciated by the employees and the public generally. Everybody was welcome and everybody had a big time.

The Van Lear High School news again found its way to the pages of the newspaper.

November 4, 1926—Saturday was a big day for Van Lear High. Our first winning game. This is the second year our boys have played and they certainly have shown the people of Big Sandy that Van Lear is on the map in football.

The Tigers of Paintsville was the team defeated. Our Bank Mules proved that they had a kick that won. Our boys went out with the determination to win, and nothing could have prevented it, for they fought to the finish. Red Lynn made two touchdowns and Elmer Price made one. He sure is a star at football if he is small. At first it looked as though the Tigers would eat us up but we proved the better fighters. The score was 19-13.

We hope this means victory for us in the games to come and the school means to back our boys and help them in every way possible. Elizabeth Kemper and Art McCoart were elected yell leaders and they (with Miss Shaw) kept the team peppy throughout the game.

Paintsville Hospital Notes listed a tragic mine accident.

November 4, 1926—Terry Jones of Van Lear, was admitted to the hospital Thursday night with a badly lacerated hand as a result of a mine injury. It was necessary to amputate his left thumb.

Late in 1926, a killing occurred in Van Lear.

November 25, 1926—Charles Harris, a colored man of Van Lear, who shot to death Joe Symansky at that place a few weeks ago, was sentenced to ten years in the penitentiary when tried in the Johnson Circuit Court last week. Symansky was a Pole and both men were miners employed by the Consolidation Coal Company of Van Lear.

The testimony showed that the Negro and the Pole had quarreled over the affections of a Negro woman who was at the home of another Negro miner, and the shooting followed which resulted in Symansky's death.

The prosecution was conducted by the Commonwealth's Attorney Tobe Wiley. The defense was represented by attorneys F. P. Blair and J. L. Harrington of this city.

A train vs. automobile accident at the Van Lear crossing killed one, injured two.

December 16, 1926—Monday morning, a Ford taxi, driven by L. E. Haynes, with Pete Zino and Eugene Compton, as passengers, was completely demolished, when struck by passenger train No. 37.

Zino, his wife and baby had arrived on the Van Lear train and were en route to Wolf Pitt where he was to take charge of the club house at that place. He discovered while waiting for the passenger train at West Van Lear that he had left the key to his suitcase at Van Lear and he employed Haynes to drive him back for the key, while Compton, a young man, was also in the car. As the car neared the crossing above the depot, Zino said he saw the passenger train coming and warned Haynes repeatedly but Haynes said he could beat the train. But just as the Ford was in the middle of the track, the train struck it.

All three men were brought to the Paintsville Hospital where it was found that Haynes and Compton received slight bruises but Zino was seriously injured. He died Tuesday morning and the remains were shipped to Tennessee for burial. He made a statement before he died that he tried to keep Haynes from crossing the track but he refused to heed the warning.

Haynes has been arrested for operating a taxi without a license.

The governor came to town to speak to the graduating seniors.

May 12, 1927—Governor W. J. Fields will deliver the commencement address at the Van Lear High School graduation exercises Monday evening, May 16, at the Recreation Hall. Tickets are now on sale and only those who have tickets will be admitted. Seats are being rapidly taken and those who desire to attend should call at the Recreation Hall and purchase tickets. Those at a distance may call by phone and have seats reserved.

This establishes a precedent for the Big Sandy Valley, for as far as we know, this is the first time the chief executive of Kentucky has ever delivered a graduation address.

The address of the governor, it is expected, will draw a large crowd of out-of-town visitors to Van Lear.

There's nothing mentioned about the price of a ringside seat, but the citizens of Van Lear were treated to some boxing and wrestling, thanks to Consol.

July 23, 1927—A boxing show and wrestling match will be held at Van Lear Saturday evening, July 30, at 7:30, in which the people of this section will be entertained with the manly arts of boxing and wrestling in which five contests are scheduled.

Preliminary and semi-final bouts will be held first preparatory to the main bout, an eight-round boxing contest between Howard Smith, of Russell, Ky., and George Hamm, of Huntington, W. Va. After the main bout, a wrestling match will be staged between Paul RuLong of Paintsville and Leo Moore of Minnesota.

These boxing shows are sponsored by Maj. E. G. Wells, employment manager of The Consolidation Coal Company at Van Lear, and furnish clean sport for the people of this section.

A fatality was reported at the Consolidation Coal Company mine.

September 22, 1927—Wm Hall of West Van Lear was killed in the mines of the Consolidation Coal Company at Van Lear, Ky., September 17, 1927.

He was the adopted son of Rev. James L. Hall and Martha Hall of Meally, Ky. He was born March 25, 1883 and passed into the great beyond Sept. 17, 1927. He leaves a widowed wife and two children, a boy and a girl, and a host of friends and relatives to mourn his passing.

The family circle has been broken and a chair has been made vacant that can never be filled. He accepted Christ about seven years ago and for the last twelve months has been a strict member of the Church of Christ at West Van Lear and was a member of the church board. He was strictly loved and always stood for the right; he was big hearted and kind to all.

He could always be depended on. In his death, the community has lost one of its best citizens, the church a staunch member, the widow a good husband, the children a kind father. He has gone where the just never die.

The funeral was conducted by the Rev. L. H. Parker, pastor of the Christen Church at Paintsville. The funeral was attended by the largest crowd that ever attended a funeral at Van Lear.

The society page reporter stayed busy.

November 10, 1927—The Boy Scouts had a show at the Van Lear Theater on October 27 for the purpose of making money to buy uniforms for the Scouts. They realized about $65. Another show will be given sometime during this month.

The Scouts met on Tuesday night and organized five patrols and elected patrol leaders. At the regular meeting they are to choose a name for the patrols. These boys are organizing a basketball team and will soon be ready to meet any scout team on the Big Sandy River.

The following Van Lear teachers are attending E.K.E.A. this week at Ashland: Misses Mildred Bush, Garnett Napier, Ruth Dickerson, Elva Fields, Naoma Wells, Elizabeth Gifford, Kitty Bess Dodson, Clara Shaw, Mrs. Russell Kelley, Mrs. Ewing Wells, Mrs. C. V. Snapp, Harry Burchett and C. V. Snapp.

The Paintsville Herald reported the obituary of a mine fatality.

March 8, 1928—Luther Shearer, machinist at number four mine, was killed instantly Saturday, about 12:30 p.m. when slate fell along the main entry as Mr. Shearer was coming out of the mine. Mr. Shearer was a well-liked man, and very popular with the people with whom he worked, so his death came as a great shock to his friends. He leaves, besides his wife, four sons: Homer, Angus, Malcolm and Ernest, and a daughter, Dorothy.

Those from out of town who attended the funeral were his mother, stepfather and a brother from Wayland.

The funeral was held at the Baptist Church Monday afternoon at 1 o'clock after which interment took place in the Van Lear Cemetery.

A nice article ran in 1928 extolling the achievements of a Van Lear service man.

April 19, 1928—Elbert McCoy, of Van Lear, Johnson County, who is a Petty Officer in the Navy, has just received his second commendation from the Navy Department for exceptionally meritorious conduct.

The official letter of commendation says, in part: "— these men (McCoy and Gowan) were transferred here to assist as subject of certain air tests in connection with Navy Project F-100-0 the influence of varying oxygen on the effects of noxious percentages of CO_2 in submarines. They were subjects of a considerable number of these experiments. The situation was distinctly uncomfortable for them, in some instances actually involving physical strain. They not only cooperated cheerfully as subjects, but showed an interest and a spirit of helpfulness in the work which was very gratifying. It is felt that their services should have distinctive recognition."

Mr. McCoy was previously commended by the Secretary of the Navy of January 25, 1924 for "their heroic efforts above and beyond the call of duty, to serve the life of John Andrew, Water Tender First Class, U.S. Navy, who died as the result of a fall from the top of Pali, a sheer precipice on the northern side of Hawaii."

Mr. McCoy enlisted on July 9, 1920, and re-enlisted in 1924 on the day following his discharge. He is now a member of the crew of the submarine S-20. He has a brother, Herman McCoy, now living at Van Lear.

Mid-summer saw some important visitors to the Overnight City.

September 13, 1938—Mr. George Anderson, newly-elected president of the Consolidation Coal Co., accompanied by his wife and several other people connected with the company, arrived in Van Lear Monday morning on a special train.

A dinner was served at the club house on Monday evening to the heads of the different departments of the company and their wives, in honor of Mr. Anderson. From seven to nine o'clock, a reception was given at the Recreation Building that the employees of the company might be able to meet Mr. Anderson.

As was proven by Mr. Charles Feutter, sometimes a Rotary meeting serves unexpected purposes.

October 4, 1928—A very interesting meeting of the Paintsville-Van Lear Rotary Club was held at Van Lear last Tuesday and the luncheon was served at the club house there. Many of the good women of that progressive city helped with the luncheon and the entertainment. Our good friend Charles Feutter presided in the absence of President Paul B. Hall and the hour was pleasantly spent.

Mr. Snyder, manager of the Millers Creek Division of the Consolidation Coal Company, made a short talk in which he welcomed the visitors and said we should get together more often. He spoke complimentary of the club and its work. Bill Hess, who always helps entertain visitors that visit Van Lear, was on the program. He told two very interesting stories and sang a beautiful solo. While not a member of the club, Bill has a good friend in each Rotarian.

Charles Feutter said we Paintsville people were rare visitors in Van Lear except on paydays. Charles wants these two towns to visit each other more often and he is right.

More of the club meetings should be held at Van Lear when the roads get better and more and more of the Van Lear citizens should belong to the club.

It might be interesting to again call attention to the fact that the slip in the Mayo Trail between Paintsville and Van Lear has been named the "Charles Feutter Slip," because of the interest shown by him in getting it repaired. Many of the club members have been wondering if it could be possible that he arranged the meeting of the club on Tuesday for the purpose of bringing the club members over this slip on a rainy day to get them more interested in having a better road between the two towns. He certainly made converts out those who have been lacking in interest along those lines. "Keeping everlastingly at it brings success," is Mr. Feutter's motto in getting a road between Paintsville and Van Lear and if a few other citizens would display as much interest as he has displayed, we will soon have this road.

A week later, the following article appeared.

October 11, 1928—At a meeting of the Paintsville-Van Lear Rotary Club Tuesday afternoon in the Mayo Memorial Church, Hon. James W. Turner, who has been working for the past several months on the matter of paved road to Van Lear made the principal talk. Mr. Turner said that he had been successful in getting the state highway commission to agree to take over this road as soon as it was completed and that it would be maintained by the state and federal governments. This section of road is only about one-half mile in length but it is the worst section of road in the county.

It will connect with the paved road of the Mayo Trail at Dawkins and extend to the bridge in West Van Lear. At the bridge it will connect with a new paved road the Consolidation Coal Company proposes to build at their own expense. This will provide a paved road from Paintsville to Van Lear, passable at all seasons of the year.

Mr. Turner said that road contractors who had their machinery now in this section could be induced, and in fact, had agreed, to build this road and hard surface it for approximately ten thousand dollars. The Consolidation Coal Company, or the city of Van Lear, will donate to the county the sum of twenty-eight thousand dollars on this road; in addition to building at their own expense the road from the bridge to the city of Van Lear.

This matter was discussed at length by the members of the club, and it was unanimously decided to call a mass meeting of the citizens of these two towns to meet with the fiscal court and all other organizations who want good roads.

Then the next week, another article on the subject appeared.

October 18, 1928—At a meeting of citizens of the county with the Johnson County Fiscal Court last Monday, the paved road at Van Lear was discussed and engineers from the Northeast Coal Company and the Consolidation Coal Company, at no expense to the county, made the survey of the new road and blue prints of the proposed road are now ready for inspection.

There is said to be a little trouble ahead about the right-of-way and some argument about which street will be used through the town of West Van Lear.

These matters should in no way prevent this road from being built this fall. Now is the time to build the road. Contractors claim the road can be graded and hard surfaced in six weeks. The road connects with the Mayo Trail paving at Dawkins and with the new hard surfaced road to be built by the Consolidation Coal Company.

The Johnson County Fiscal Court and the citizens of the county will make a serious mistake if they allow this road to go over until next spring to be built. The time to build the road is now and it can be done if everybody interested will keep right after it until the contractors go to work.

It is going to take fast work to get it completed before winter and the sooner we get it started the better it will be for all people concerned.

November 8, 1928—The local Rotary Club spent most of the hour at the regular meeting Tuesday in discussing the Mayo Trail at Dawkins to Van Lear Bridge, a distance of about one mile. The county had already appropriated the money to build the road but made it necessary for the citizens to secure the right-of-way.

James W. Turner, who has had the work in charge some time, made his report that the right-of-way was now secured but that funds were necessary to pay for same.

The club voted that the Kiwanis Club be asked to join in the movement to secure at once the necessary cash and that the county is allowed to place the contract for the work this week. It is estimated that the work of building and hard surfacing this road would require about three weeks and the machinery is already on the ground waiting for the orders from the fiscal court.

Tuesday afternoon the committee, composed of Tobe Rule, W. H. Slone and Frank Conley, started the work and in a short time had the required amount of cash to finish the payments on the right-of-way and the matter is now in the hands of the county for the order to start the work.

Unfortunately, 1929 began with another killing in the community. As are all the articles in this book, the following story is just as it appeared in the paper.

January 10, 1929—James Music, age 44, a miner, was shot and instantly killed at Van Lear last week, and two youths, Everett Brickley, 16, and Langley Ratliff, 14, were arrested and charged with the killing. Young Brickley is a son of Ed Brickley, while the Ratliff boy is a son of Rev. Earnie Ratliff.

According to testimony adduced at the examining trial held before Magistrate I. L. Auxier, Judge pro tem, Saturday, the boys were out shooting with a .22 rifle near the Music home. They were shooting at sycamore balls on a tree near the home of the miner and fearing that a stray bullet might to deflected and hit some member of his family, Music went out and asked the boys not to shoot near his home as they might accidentally injure someone, and the boys, it is said, became incensed and declared they would shoot him, and suited the action to their words. Brickley, it is said, then took deliberate aim at Mr. Music's head and fired, the bullet striking him in the right temple, ranging upward shattering the skull and entering the brain.

The principal witnesses against the defendants were the10-year-old son of Mr. Music and a Dale boy, who gave a pathetic, though straightforward, account of the unfortunate affair. Music's son said the family had all been stricken with flu, the elder Music being weak from the disease had sat down on a rock and while in this position, the boy fired the fatal shot. The man pitched forward on his face. The son placed his hat under his head and went for help. He was taken to his home where he died one hour later.

The Music boy's account of the killing was corroborated by the Dale boy who was an eye witness to the tragedy.

Mr. Music was a hardworking, inoffensive man, and the father of a big family who are left in bad circumstances by reason of the father's death.

Young Brickley was held to the action of the grand jury under $2,500 bond. The Ratliff boy, who is 14 years old, was tried before Mr. Auxier Tuesday and was exonerated of the charge as the proof showed he was only with the Brickley boy and took no actual part in the killing of the miner.

In March of that year, a Van Lear man announces his bid for a political office.

March 14, 1929—The man who wins the nomination of Jailer of Johnson County at the August primary, will be opposed by a Democrat and a strong man, according to J. W. Messer of Van Lear, who this week authorized the *Herald* to announce his candidacy for the office of Jailer. He is the first man to announce on the Democratic ticket this year and expects the nomination without opposition but will make a vigorous campaign to win over his Republican opponent in the November election.

Mr. Messer is 45 years of age and for 32 years has followed the occupation of a miner. For the past 14 years he has been located at Van Lear, where he had been a valuable and honored employee of the Consolidation Coal Company. In placing his announcement, Mr. Messer said that he was a laboring man and had always earned his bread by the sweat of his face and would make an especial appeal to the working classes and especially to the miners of the county. He further stated that if elected, which he firmly believed he would be, he would strive with all this strength and ability to make the people a good Jailer. He promised if elected he would attend strictly to the affairs of his own office and nothing more, and that he believed that the office of Jailer required service pertaining to the jail and the jail property and that prisoners entrusted to his care should occupy his sole attention.

He goes into the campaign with a good recommendation as he has the backing of his neighbors, and this alone is as good a recommendation as any man can have. Besides being a popular man, he is prominently connected in lodge circles, being a Mason, an Odd Fellow and a Red Man.

And yet another Van Lear man is involved in a killing.

May 9, 1929—For the second time in two weeks, Prestonsburg suffered the loss of a police officer when

George Horn, age 55, was shot and almost instantly killed while attempting to arrest three men last Saturday night who were charged with being drunk and disorderly. The men were Alonzo Blair and his son of West Van Lear and "Tad" Anderson of Van Lear. Anderson is charged with the fatal shooting of officer Horn. Blair and his son had no connection with the killing, merely being members of the party when the fatal shooting occurred. They were given an examining trial at Prestonsburg, fined for drunkenness and were released. Anderson is held in the Prestonsburg jail without bond.

Anderson is a native of Magoffin County but has been at Van Lear for a number of years where he has worked as a miner.

The shooting occurred near the C & O depot where the three men are said to have been drunk and disorderly. It is said that the three men had driven their car across the bridge and then upon the platform of the depot.

The Police Judge of Prestonsburg ordered their arrest and Chief of Police Griffith, together with Horn went to the scene of trouble to make the arrest. Blair and his son, it is said, submitted peacefully and were in charge of Chief Griffith, but Anderson tried to get away and ran a short distance where officer Horn began firing at him and called to him to halt. It is alleged that Anderson told Horn to stop shooting and he would surrender. As the officer approached, Anderson whipped out a gun and shot the officer twice. One bullet took effect in the arm and the other through the heart.

Anderson then attempted to make his getaway but was captured near Cliff, a mile below Prestonsburg. Officers report that Anderson was in possession of a gun when arrested with four empty shells in the chambers

And in the November election, Van Lear's John Messer is elected.

November 7, 1929—By a large majority, John Messer, of Van Lear, the Democratic candidate for Jailer, won in Tuesday's election over George W. Spears, the Republican nominee.

Chapter Three: 1930-1939

*T*he thirties proved tragic for many families of Van Lear miners as the paper reported several fatalities for the Consolidation Mining Company, with nine men dying in one explosion.

On top of all that, two suicides were reported, along with another homicide, and one young Van Lear man was killed by a train.

The bright side of the news, however, included an article about the movies coming to the overnight city, a story about the excellent performance of Consol's mine safety team, and a report of the opening of two new filling stations.

A series of reports done by a group of brilliant sixth graders told the history of Van Lear, and many stories of the Van Lear High School football team were printed during the thirties.

There was the occasional obituary of an important Van Lear resident, reports of activities of the Van Lear police department, and what we like to refer to as "court house news." We found the story interesting regarding the young man who was acquitted of the charge of biting off the thumb of a police officer. There was also a report of the pardon of the mine inspector who had been charged with negligence in the explosion that took nine miners' lives in July, 1935.

It was a pretty big deal, especially for the youngsters, when talking movies came to Van Lear.

July 17, 1930—The progressive town of Van Lear opened its first new talking picture show last Tuesday evening. They have remodeled their theatre building, elevated the seats and installed new R. C. A. Photophone talking equipment.

Officials of the Consolidation Coal Company from Jenkins were present at the opening Tuesday evening.

The Safety Team from Consolidation Coal took three prizes at the Safety Meeting held at Pikeville.

September 11, 1930—First Aid teams of the Consolidation Coal Company of Van Lear carried off three of the six prizes in the second annual safety day meeting held in Pikeville recently.

The Van Lear team, in charge of Captain H. McCarthy, took first honors with which went the Mine Safety Appliance Company cup. This cup went to the team and in addition each member of the team was awarded a small cup and Red Cross and National Safety Council medals.

Another Consolidation Coal Company team took second honors. This team was from the Jenkins operation of the same company and was in charge of H. C. Blankenship, captain.

Another Consolidation Coal Company entry from Van Lear, under Captain H. D. Wells, won sixth place.

Much interest was manifested in the First Aid meetings this year and it is estimated that four or five thousand people were present in Pikeville and witnessed the demonstrations.

Forty-six teams participated in the exhibitions this year. Fifty-six teams had originally entered but a number of them failed to appear or withdrew before contests began.

And the social life continued to be reported.

November 6, 1930—Mr. and Mr. Conroy Conley of this place gave a card and radio party Saturday evening in honor of their guests, Mr. and Mrs. Bill Witten of Oil Springs. Those present were Miss Fay Long, Jewel Marie Long, Ethel Mae Trusty, Thelma P. Witten, Rebecca K. Witten, Francis Witten, Margarette Magdaline Conley, Everet Holbrook, Glen McKenzie, Gus Conley and Jim Reed.

During the social hours, the guests were entertained by music, dancing and card playing. At a late hour, refreshments were served.

Miss Ethel Mae Trusty, Fay Long, Everet Holbrook and Glen McKenzie were the Sunday evening guests of Thelma Pauline Witten at Oil Springs.

Tragedy struck the community in the early fall of the next year when the Rev. Felty O'Bryan died after an illness of nine days.

September 24, 1931—Rev. Felty O'Bryan, 53, a resident of Van Lear for many years, died at his home at that place at 10:00 a.m. last Sunday morning, following an illness of nine days of pneumonia.

Rev. O'Bryan was an employee of the Consolidation Coal Company where he worked as tipple foreman during the week days and attended church, ministered to the sick and preached on Sundays. He had followed this practice for years and was very valuable to the community as well as the county generally.

He was a minister at the Old United Baptist Church, holding membership in the Cedar Grove Church of West Van Lear, and was known throughout Johnson County as one of the best men and a citizen whose private life was one worthy of emulation by younger men. His life has been spent in the service of God, his family and the church of his choice and his passing will be mourned by a large number of relatives and friends.

Short funeral services were held at the home on Monday morning in charge of Rev. Guy W. Preston and Rev. Roscoe LeMaster, brother ministers of the Baptist faith, after which the body was transported to the O'Bryan cemetery at the mouth of Pickle Fork on Barnett's Creek for its last resting place, there to await the resurrection morn, by the side of his father and mother who preceded him in death years ago. Services were held at the grave in the presence of one of the largest concourses of sorrowing relatives and friends ever seen at a burial in that section.

Besides his widow, he is survived by nine children and numerous friends and relatives throughout the county.

In the early fall of 1931, the mines at Van Lear were running six days a week.

October 8, 1931—With the approach of winter and colder weather, a general pick-up in the mining industry of the Big Sandy Valley is indicated. Mines all along the line of the C & O's Big Sandy Division have become more active in the last few weeks and the tonnage has been greatly increased. As a result, C & O trains are pulling more coal out of the valley at this date than at any other period within the past year.

The mines of the Consolidation Coal Company at Van Lear have been running full capacity for the past few weeks with indications for steady runs in the future. Last week the Van Lear mines were operated both day and night, six days a week.

The coal industry is the backbone of business in the Big Sandy Valley and with coal operations running regularly, better business throughout the valley will be the result.

During the last few months of 1931 and the first couple months of 1932, things must not have been going too well. Thus this optimistic piece ran in the paper.

February 25, 1932—Indications point to more steady work at the Van Lear mines. Business in general has started to improve and we naturally expect the coal business to improve. Soon our lake orders will be coming in and then we may look for better work.

Van Lear has not fared so badly during these dull months. It could have be a lot worse. We are given credit for having the best mining town in Kentucky, and of course, we all agree that this is true.

Van Lear is the largest town on the Big Sandy River. Our mining operation is the largest on the river. Our people are looking to the future with renewed hopes that things will soon be humming here as they did a few years ago.

Our people are all working together to advance our schools, churches, social life and all things that make a better city and community.

We can improve our city if we all cooperate.

The honor roll of the Van Lear Central School listed many excellent pupils.

February 25, 1932—Grade 1, Mrs. O. L. Risner, teacher: The following pupils have an "A" average. Frank Davis, Thomas McCourt, Jr., Billy Ratcliff, Marcus Spears, Richard Swentzel, James Elwood Vaughan, Barbara Akers, Anne Beers, Innie Baker, Minnie Caudill, Arizona Davis, Billy Gene Lewis, Flossie Music, Monnie Louise Prince, Maxine Sellards and Geneva Ward.

Second and third grades: Charles Conley, Charles Ray May, Mary Louise Daniels, Beatrice Dixon, Gladys

Hayden, Betty Jane Lambert, Alta Powers, Naomi Ruth Rucker, Loretta Burchett, Phyllis Gunning, Vencil Young, Russell Rucker, Earl Dixon, Ruth Eloise Webb and Lottie Short.

Second grade, Miss Ruth Adams teacher: Magdalene Conley, Helen Harris, Douglas Boyd, Junior Burnett, Harold Smith, Robert Jasper and Russell Rice.

Third grade, Miss Bessie Harris teacher: Earl Barker, Ernest Bowling, Johnnie Colvin, Vencil Lewis, Arlie McCallister, Estill O'Bryan, Duncan Pack, Raymond Ward, Franklin Ralph Perry, Edna Caudill, Mildred Hicks, Carrinne McCourt, Edna O'Bryan, Gloria Mae Painter, Ruby Staton, Annabel Thompson, Juanita Young, Dorothy Lambert, Lorene Stratton and Virginia Riffe.

Fourth grade, Miss Doris Hobson teacher: Elmer Adams, Dwight Barron, Roger Feutter, Jackie Hunter, Earl Preston, Russell May, Warren Picklesimer, Nick Savko, Wayne Salyers, Robert Smith, Billy Snipes, Morris VanHoose, Jimmie Ward. D.B. Williams, Evelyn Hitchcock, Jeannette Mace, Evelyn Music, Irvine Spears, Arlie Spradlin and Lorene Ward.

Fifth grade, Miss Lenore Hall, teacher: Charlene Adams, Marie Ealey, Margie Gaiski, Stella Gaiski, Elizabeth Russell, Celia Stapleton, Dorothy Wells, Golda Hall, Garner Daniel, Lloyd Daniel, Wilbur Music, and Raymond Young.

Fifth grade, Mrs. Alka M. Gibson, teacher: Irene Adams, Mae Bowling, Irene Castle, Lorene Conley, Ethel Hall, Irene Lewis, Beatrice Phelps, Florence Riffe, Mary Rucker, Evelyn Selvage, Daisy Thompson, Georgia

Young, Gearl Cordell, Clarence Fairchilds, Eugene Mace, Troy Nunnery, John Pack, Charles Ratcliff, Jr., John Lambert, and Lewis Mickles.

Between March 3 and April 7, 1932, The Herald published a history of Van Lear which was researched and written by the Van Lear Central School sixth graders.

March 3, 1932—History of Van Lear, Chapter 1

We would like to have camped on the hill upon which we are now gazing twenty-three or twenty-four years ago. We imagine wild flowers bloomed in abundance.

The blended fragrance of Rhododendrons, violets, honeysuckles, butter-cups and dandelions would have filled one's nostrils.

When night closed in upon us, possibly we could have heard old Sir Reynard as he ran through the woods in search of food, or the yelping of the hounds as they went after him in hot pursuit. We might have heard the howling of the wolf, the shrill notes of the wild cat, or the soft treads of the opossum, coon or skunk.

We imagine that we would have needed no alarm clock to arouse us from our slumber; the voice of the Blue Jay as he winged his way through the heavens, the sweet refrains of the wren and the gold finches, songs of the Cardinals, and robins would have been sufficient to cause us to open our eyes. Then we could have seen old Sol in all his dazzling splendor painting fields and brooks with a brilliant hue. Had we lowered our gaze to the valley, we could have seen the bare-footed mountain lassie as she drove Old Jersey to a small pasture not far away.

In a nearby clearing, Brother Sam was doing his share as he followed old Jack to and fro through the field preparatory for a corn crop in the future. Father took out the grubs, lifted the roots and stumps from the ground, piled and burned the brush. Mother, after preparing the morning meal, gathered the dirty clothes and washed them in the nearby stream. Joe, who was the laziest member of the family, possibly said, "I don't feel like working today, so I think I'll saunter into the woods and bring home a few squirrel."

In this brief description, we would not forget to mention that little building with the overshot wheel, down by the old mill stream. There, on rainy days, men gathered with their grists and discussion of weather, crops, hunting and fishing took first place as the current events of the day. We were about to say the family troubles and quarrels made up a part of the conversation, but we know enough about the good old mountaineers to know they had few troubles and what they did have, they were men and women enough to keep to themselves.

Oh, how we would like to have journeyed here for just a few months anyway, in a land of paradise where the beauty of nature reigned supreme and where one could have at least killed one rabbit, squirrel or quail. We would like to have lingered on these scenes; however, progress willed it, that we pass on in our narration to other things.

During the period of which we have been speaking, there were possibly a dozen or more houses in the vicinity of Miller's Creek, or what is now known as Van Lear.

Upon this site where our central school building now stands, there was once a house, post office and store. This was known as the "Richmond Place." James Richmond was postmaster and James H. Hall, who is the father of one of our present sixth graders, delivered mail. Just south of this place, a house sat back in a cave and was inhabited by John Music. This is possibly the reason that this hollow bears that name today.

March 10, 1932—Chapter II

We make no apology for copying after our friend Lowell Thomas in skipping here and there to give you detailed accounts of the various houses that were located on hills and dales, for our readers must know that we constitute a class, possibly not the best in the world for the grade, and by no means the worst class. Therefore, we will endeavor to name and locate several more buildings with their inhabitants.

Then, too, we have historical names of various hollows here about, which cannot be overlooked by any means. "Wolf Pen Hollow" got its name (so we have heard) from a pen or trap being built in order that the inhabitants might free the country of wolves, which were pests and deadly enemies of farm animals and fowl. The name was given to this place possibly sixty or seventy years ago. We do not have a record that Phelps, Atkins, or any others who lived there twenty to thirty years ago, ever killed any wolves. We feel reasonably sure that there are no wolves there today, for we have strolled along the hillside several times without seeing even a share. Another place known for its sweetness flowing from the hillside, caused from Burges and DeLong raising so much cane, is "Sorghum Hollow."

The Number Two bath house (just back of the present Recreation Building) now stands where was once an old institution of learning. This was a one-room school (according to the information we have) where the principal subjects of leaning were reading, writing and arithmetic, given by teachers who emphasized their words with the sound of the hickory limb, and these were taken by the boys and girls who were unable to stand the gaff of them all. Some of the sorghum spoken of above might have found its way into the school room. Whether or not it sweetened the disposition of the school master and mistress we don't know. We know that we, who are writing this, wish that our teacher would sometimes eat some jelly or molasses.

Happy Hollow (which is the one to your right if you face the front of the present Methodist church) received its name from the Happy family. We have the name of John Happy, who lived in this hollow.

The left hand hollow from the Methodist church (if you face it the same way) is known as Webb Hollow. From the information we have, this hollow has been inhabited by the Webbs for forty-five years. We have had the pleasure of knowing those who live there today. We are classmates of one, and have had to prepare hard lessons and have our coats dusted by another one.

Oh, Boy! What a mistake it would have been had we gone without mentioning "Dot possum in de simmon tree" (in the head of a hollow which now bears its name?) So far we have been unable to get the names of any persons who lived in Opossum Hollow before the building of our camp.

Hitchcock School House, Akers and No. One Hollows all figure in our present town life. The first two received their names from men who lived there probably three or four decades ago. No. One Hollow is near Mine No. 151, thus the name. The other one of this immediate list received its name by a certain building where knowledge reigns supreme and where statements as "hit ain't gonna ran no more," "this here ain't no place to sleep," etc. have been thrown into the waste basket to become part of a forgotten lore. School House Hollow was named after the camp started and was named for the building erected at the mouth of it.

By and by there came a time when the beauties of nature were changed. The stealthy treads of animals, songs of birds chirping, of crickets on their E Flat cornets, and katydids playing trombone solos all changed from peaceful notes to screams and sounds of fear. This was because men had come to change a thing of beauty into that which would be more profitable to their needs.

The purchase of hundreds of acres of timber and mineral land by the Consolidation Coal Company was the first step toward the real history of our town. The purchase was followed (we imagine) by numerous meetings, consultations on the part of officials, engineers, geologists, carpenters and laborers, and figured in the change that was soon to come. Timber men with sharpened tools went forth into the forest to make ready the logs for the mills. Teamsters were there to take them away. In the valley below saws hummed as they ate their way through the logs.

March 24, 1932—Chapter 3

The days of quietude for the natives of Millers Creek were over. The slapping of boards together, rattling of wagons, voices of mule drivers, sawing and nailing of carpenters sounded and resounded throughout the atmosphere from early dawn till late at night.

We suppose that the first buildings to be erected were an office building, a club house and a house for the general manager. The first office building was located near the old power house and was practically the same size as the present one. The general manager's house and the club houses were located on the hill south of the old power house. John J. Smith was the first manager. The following are some of the first office men: J. D. Rogers, chief engineer; Walter Shunk, chief electrician; Jonathan Jenkins, superintendent; James Price, auditor. Mrs. Donta was first matron of the club house on the hill. The others were Mrs. McNew, Mrs. Dixon and Mrs. Stump. The club house on the hill burned in February 1922, and the present club house was built the same year. We do not know the first three matrons or the success accorded them, however, we do know the one who is in charge of the club house now and we feel that she is the woman for the place. We all owe her much gratitude and respect.

The following are those who have held the highest positions in the camp: J.C. Gillette, C. F. Smith, J.M. Lee, Garner Fletcher, E.R. Price, and J.D. Snyder. This position calls for a man with an unusual amount of good common sense, high ideas, and whose character is above reproach with regard to his dealings with those who are subject to his will. This position also calls for a man with high social ability. Having known Mr. Price and Mr. Snyder, we are prepared to say that they are above reproach.

The medical staff in our camp should be placed among those of highest honor. It is a given that human beings are subject to physical defects and we are so constituted that disease germs may prey on our systems to the extent of permanent disability of certain parts of our structure and also death itself may result. These conditions are greatly altered by the advice, knowledge, service and medicine of our doctors.

Those who have administered to our physical wants, alleviated pain and robbed old monster Death of many of us for the past two decades are Dr. Bill Gamble, Dr. Crate Gamble, Dr. Johnson, Dr. Holbrook, Dr. Davis, Dr. Row, Dr. Lyon, Dr. Sutton, Dr. Spencer, Dr. Price, Dr. Munn, and Dr. O.L. Spencer. We have had the pleasure of knowing only two of these intimately and some of us owe them, not only for alleviating pain, but for our lives as well. We would, indeed be ungrateful if we did not render them the highest esteem.

The Public Health nurses are Misses Boyd, Bean, Beavers and Love. Some of us do not realize the importance of this position. However, we know that they, as members of the medical staff, are interested in our health and growth. They employ methods and means to this end about which many know very little. Those who receive their instructions commit errors and omit things they should do thus making it hard for them to carry out their program. We do not doubt that through their tireless efforts and watchful care, a stronger, healthier womanhood and manhood will result. Miss Beavers and Miss Love, who are in our community today, have spent hours trying to get us to do things that will help us to become stronger. Then we know that without them we would possibly grow careless about taking care of our bodies.

The last, but not least, on the medical staff is the dentist. Doctors and nurses tell us that decayed teeth will poison our system to the extent that we may become physical wrecks if we do not have the defects remedied. Dr. Wolfe knows the ills of the teeth and how to combat the forces that work to destroy our teeth. No one has worked harder to bring about a stronger manhood and womanhood that Dr. Wolfe. Many times he has visited our schools and made talks regarding our teeth that will have a lasting effect on our community.

March 11, 1932—Chapter 4

In last week's issue we gave the names of several of the main men and women of our camp. In this issue, we aim to include the chief leaders of all other departments.

General superintendents: Jonathan Jenkins, J. D. Rogers and Wm. Gunning.

Chief engineers: J. D. Rogers, F. A. Vockradt, J. J. Fleech, Wm. Gunning and B. H. Atkinson.

Foremen, Mine No. 1: E.D. Easterling, Bill Adams, Geo. Griffith, Jerry Hager, John Estel, Jim Bob Worlin, Con Daniels and E. L. Lambert.

Foremen, Mine No. 2: Buck Smith, John Estep, Grover Wolf, Hillary Lewis, Earnest Layan and John Hammond.

Foremen, Mine No. 3: A. J. Johnson, Bill Henson, Joe Sennat, Lee Wilbur, E. L. Lambert, Chris Boles, Pat Courier and James Hall.

Foremen, Mine No. 4 Joe Madison, W. M. Adams, Joe Sennat, Bill Harrison, Frank Addis, George Wolfe, Ed Cecil and E. L. Lambert.

Foremen, Mine No. 5: Jerry Hager, Ed Cecil, Hillary Lewis, Jim Wollin, John Helton and Con Daniel.

Chief Electrician: Charlie Feutter.

Store Managers: McDaniels, Michaels, P. L. Hughes, Paul Ashcraft, J. M. Weekly and E. H. Cundiff.

Recreation Managers: G. C. Chamber, Major Wells, P. M. Randall and C. D. Barron.

B and CI Department Chiefs: Joe Williamson, Tobe Fairchild and L. M. Griffin.

Superintendents of Schools: Conley, Congleton, George, Bell, Snapp and Reed.

Then last, but not least, comes the man whose duty is to watch over all members of the camp for the best interest of all concerned—the Personnel Men: Major Wells and A. B. McGary.

Time and space do not permit us to give the names of all those who have contributed to the progress of our camp. The names which we have given above are the leading men in each department from the time the camp started to the present day. The office forces and assistants of each department and the host of teachers, who have labored to bring about greater progress and a better community, cannot be mentioned here. Nevertheless, their works may be seen everywhere.

We have failed to mention the multitudes that have had the strength and the nerve to bring hundreds of thousands of tons of coal from beneath the surface. Let us say (just here) that those men are to be admired for their bravery. Without them, there would be no coal operations and the human race would have to discover something else to use for fuel.

We have stated in a former issue that on the grounds of our present surroundings there was once a wilderness. The timber was used to build homes for the workers. Plumbing, heating and electric equipment had to be installed. A sanitary water system was provided. All these and more were provided for those who had to labor here.

The railroad, upon which our coal was to be transported to main lines, was built in the year of 1908-1909. This line was also used to convey passengers back and forth from No. 5 to the Junction until about three years ago when our road was constructed.

April 7, 1932—Chapter 5

We shall not attempt to follow up the improvements of each department of our company here at Millers Creek. However, it is a major policy of the company to progress each year.

When the mines were first opened, bringing the coal to the surface was a slow process as it had to be dug and hauled out with small mules and ponies. With the advent of modern machinery and modern methods such as transporting with motors and better cars, we would say that production is twice and possibly three times as great as it was in the time of the pony express.

The fads and fashions of each succeeding year have influenced the merchandise departments to the extent that there has been a change in buildings, an increased stock of goods and efficiency in handling them.

The first picture shows in Van Lear were in tents and possibly in a little room on the ground floor under the present Community Hall. Sometime later the Recreation Building was erected which provided for a nice theatre with silent pictures. Today we have the benefit of the talkies under a management which is hard to beat.

We suppose too, that in the early days when there were no roads the doctors had to go on horseback or walk. Also medical equipment and supplies were not as adequate as today when anyone in our camp is able to get a doctor in ten minutes.

Our present central school building was formerly not as large as it is today and was used only for the grades. Later, other rooms were added and it was also used for high school pupils.

There were three buildings in the camps: Number Five, Central and Lower River School. Approximately five years ago a new high school building was erected. Two years ago the Lower School was vacated and the pupils were sent to Central School. Now, our school system consists of three buildings and a staff of a superintendent and seventeen teachers who are putting forth every effort to train those who are under their care to become citizens of which their community may be proud.

The last two decades have witnessed innumerable changes. This town sprang up in a night, as it were. Each succeeding day brought changes both in physical and personal features. The working system is somewhat like that of our government in that it is divided into so many departments with separate and distinct powers, each keeping check on the other to some extent with higher authorities who are over all.

We may say in conclusion that we are proud of the fact that we are living here. Our company officials are proud of us. They realize that someday we will have to step into their tracks and carry on the work. Therefore, they are interested in our health, education and our social training. We, on our part, are interested in the growth of the town.

We have taken enough interest to gather the information which has gone into our narrative. We have made a resolution that we shall study the practical things in school that will enable us to carry on and keep step with the advancing age and that we shall never let the flag trail in the dust with reference to the activities of our quiet, peaceful little town.

(The End)

Sixth Grade Class, Van Lear Central School.

Still obviously proud of its football team, the Bank Mules continued to receive a lot of coverage in the press.

March 3, 1932—Coach Holland's Brigade of warriors began its spring football practice Monday, February 22. About 23 boys reported for practice and Coach Holland seemed well pleased with their first workouts. Although the 1932 line-up will be without six veterans of the senior class, Van Lear expects to turn out fully as good a team as last year. The Flash, Virgil Burkett, who was elected captain for 1932, is expected to run wild as usual and probably make "Twenty Grand" look like a has been.

Russell Goble, Van Lear's witty quarterback, whose sensational punts pulled the Bank Mules out of many a tight place in 1931, is again expected to display his wares. Two other backs assisting these two heroes of the gridiron will be Meade, a shifty little halfback, and Jack Campigotto, a promising rookie.

Van Lear will have its small but scrapping line as in years past, which many large and fearful teams have failed to penetrate. Those reporting for practice are Goble, Burkett, Meade, Sparks, Shearer, Fairchild, Brickley, Stapleton, Kazee, Dixon, Colvin, Cantrell,

Preston, Burchwell, Hall, Harris, Childers, Ealy, Daniels, Spradlin and Campigotto.

To Coach Holland, we wish to extend our praises for the winning team of 1931 and wish him even more success in 1932.

After an apparent lull, business was picking up.

May 26, 1932—The mines at Van Lear operated four days last week and possibly will run four days this week. This is a better run than they have had for several weeks past.

Summer months, as a rule, are better months than the winter months for coal mining here and it is hoped that the mines will have better runs for the summer.

Miners are more interested in gardening and farming this year and most every family has a garden and many are raising crops.

September 5, 1932—The Consolidation Coal Company worked six days under the hill last week. Twelve train loads of coal were hauled out of Millers Creek. The C & O roundhouse which has been closed down since the middle of July, called back six hundred men last Monday morning for work in the Russell shops.

A new business is always good for a thriving community.

September 22, 1932—Two new filling stations have been opened during the past week. Jack Goble (formerly, an attendant of J. N. Meeks Service Stations) has installed a new station of his own in Van Lear Junction, farther up toward the east. Earl Messer and Rolland Burchwell have re-opened their station.

And even when they didn't mean to be, the law was on the job.

December 1, 1932—A very cunning act on behalf of Jesse Fairchild, constable, and Buddy Castle, marshal, caused three would-be prisoners to abandon their car and flee.

Last week the two officers had arrested a man and were on their way to Paintsville when they noticed a car just ahead bearing a Tennessee license plate.

The two officers kept well up with the car, all unaware of anything. The men occupying the car thought Castle and Fairchild were trailing them. West of the Narrows, the men shut off their engine, opened the door and fled. The officers investigated and as a reward found and took from the car several pints of red liquor.

The car was brought to West Van Lear which may be advertised later to find the owner.

Someone needed to carry the mail.

July 13, 1933—Bert Young was the lowest bidder in the proposed mail carrying route between Van Lear Jct. depot and the post office here. Mr. Young is a miner, and works here; therefore, the Missus will have to perform the job. There were several good bidders who applied for the position, but none of these men wanted to rob man of living.

Bert Young got the job at a salary so small it's out of reason. He cannot more than make all necessary expenses; he bid $245 a year, which will give him about ten or eight dollars per month and expenses. He is handling two positions now. A man couldn't possibly live on such a small income alone and the work completely spoils the day as it takes time on duty both of morning and evening and night. The job dropped from $750 to a mere figure of $245 for a full year's work.

A Van Lear man suffered a spider bite and became very ill.

September 7, 1933—John Hall, a carpenter for the coal company, has been bedfast for a few days suffering from a bite from a poison spider. On Saturday morning, Mr. Hall was up and about his work about the house, when suddenly he felt a pain in the body and a sharp sting in the hand. He made it to the house where he pitched to the floor almost in a whirl of fits.

He was put to bed and a doctor summoned who said it was a spider bite. The victim was kept resting by hypodermics. When they were off, he was as bad as ever. His condition was no better Tuesday. A quick recovery is hoped for.

And tragedy strikes again.

October 5, 1933—Albritton Boyd, a youth of Van Lear, was killed at Offutt last Wednesday night, when crushed beneath the wheels of a coal train. He left home Wednesday morning to work, but boarded a coal train going west. He is said to have been standing on the end of the car rolling a cigarette. He lost his balance and fell beneath the wheels of the train. One leg and one arm were severed, in addition to head and internal wounds.

He is survived by his parents, Mr. and Mrs. Anderson Boyd, and several brothers and sisters.

A young miner was killed at Consolidation Coal.

August 23, 1934—Rupert Young, 30-year-old miner for the Consolidation Coal Company at Van Lear, was killed instantly as a result of a mine motor accident last Wednesday afternoon, August 15.

He is survived by his wife, his mother and father, Mr. and Mrs. Thomas Young of Van Lear.

Funeral services were held at the Cedar Grove United Baptist Church of which he was an active and devout member. The Rev. Guy W. Preston and the Rev. Roscoe Lemaster, pastors of the church at West Van Lear, conducted the services. Burial was in the family cemetery on Hoods Fork, where he was born and reared.

Mr. Young was a young man of sterling qualities and one of the most popular of the employees of the Consolidation Coal Company at Van Lear and had a wide circle of friends who joined with his family in mourning his passing.

He was married last March to Miss Neva Bayes, daughter of Mr. and Mrs. Leander Bayes.

He became a member of the Cedar Grove Church last winter and took an active part in church work during the remainder of his life.

Summer vacation ends and the school bells ring again.

September 6, 1934—The Van Lear Consolidated Schools began work for the year Tuesday, September 4, with an enrollment of approximately 700 in the grades and the high school. The faculty at this school is made up of 16 excellent teachers with a complete home economics department, a band, an organization of Camp Fire Girls, Boy Scouts and two glee clubs. The enrollment this year is an increase over last year showing a gradual growth at the Van Lear Schools as in other schools in Johnson County.

The faculty is composed of J. S. Reeds, superintendent; Jesse Holland, coach and mathematics; Mary Ellen Reeds, commercial; Miss McDowell, English; Miss Leach, history; Miss Ruth Adams, home economics. The junior high school teachers are Clara Shaw, mathematics and social science; Jane Evans, English and science.

J. L. Shepperd is principal of the grade school and teaches the sixth grade. The grade teachers are Alka Mae Gibson, fifth; Ethel Anderson, fifth; Doris Hobson, fourth; Bessie Harris, third, Ruth Adams, second; and Susie Risner, first. The grade school, located in Upper

Van Lear, is conducted by Vern Horne, principal, and Audrey Salyers.

The Van Lear schools are conducted by the town of Van Lear and have shown a remarkable growth during the past several years. A program of activities has been set out this year that is ambitious. A high school band is being conducted, and while it is augmented by several from outside the school, it is mainly made out of the students. An outstanding football team is promised this year and already practice has been started. The Camp Fire Girls and the Boy Scouts are two of the major activities and these two organizations are doing an excellent work with the students. Two glee clubs, one for girls and one for boys, have been formed and these two organizations already are working.

This summer, all but two of the teachers in the Van Lear schools attended summer schools, studying to make them more efficient in their duties. The Van Lear schools promise to have an even greater year than ever before.

The city election of 1934 found 10 running for school board.

November 8, 1934—Two local elections were held in Van Lear, Tuesday, November 6. They were to select two members for the town council and five members for the school board.

With a total of six running for councilman and 10 running for the school board, the following were named by the voters of Van Lear; Abe Goble, Paul Saunders, for councilmen, and Lawrence Hewlett, John Spears, Dan Preston, Eugene Stambaugh, and John Wilson for members of the school board.

The vote for the council candidates was as follows: Abe Goble, 259; Paul Saunders, 244; William Gunning, 85; J. A. McKay, 57; W. C. Snipes, 229; B. F. Phelps, 205.

In the school election, the vote was Lawrence Hewlett, 289; John Spears, 312; Dan Preston, 306; Eugene Stambaugh, 299; John Wilson, 257; L. M. Griffith, 195; Mrs. G. C. Stapleton, 179; W. H. Brown, 164; C. J. Feutter, 173; F. H. Price, 183.

In the city election there were three tickets with Abe Goble and Paul Saunders running under the Independent banner; Wm. Gunning and J. A. McKay under the People's ticket, and W. B. Snipes and B. F. Phelps under the Labor emblem.

The school race had two complete tickets with the first five running under one grouping and the last five under another.

In 1933, as Prohibition wound down, you could hardly pick up a newspaper or turn on the radio without hearing about another gangland killing in big cities like Boston or Chicago. In Van Lear, however, the case that captured people's imagination centered on whether a local man had bitten off a police officer's thumb.

December 14, 1933—Art McCoart, of Van Lear, who was convicted during the second week of the November Term of the Johnson Circuit Court on a charge of biting off the thumb of Officer George W. Spears, was acquitted in a second trial last week.

In the first trial, McCoart was given one year in the penitentiary on a charge of mayhem, which is the legal term for the disfiguration of another person.

The trial of the case caused quite a lot of interest and a large crowd of spectators were present and heard the trial.

The defense produced proof to show that the officer's thumb was cut with glass from the windshield of a car in which McCoart was being taken to the lock-up at Van Lear. The evidence was sufficient to convince the jury that McCoart was innocent of biting off the officer's thumb and returned a verdict to that effect.

Attorney C.F. Pace represented the defense.

The worst single tragedy in the history of Van Lear and the Consolidation Coal Company occurred in 1935.

July 18, 1935—As the *Herald* goes to press, the bodies of seven of the nine entombed miners caught in an explosion Wednesday at Mine Number Five of the Consolidation Coal Company, had been removed and rescue crews are still working at top speed to try to reach the other two. The work of the safety and rescue crews in finding the seven bodies and removing them in such good time is an indication to the efficiency of those groups. At one time, it seemed that it would take more than two days to reach the men caught after the explosion.

All seven bodies which have been recovered from the mine were brought to Paintsville funeral homes to be prepared for burial. Most to these were badly crushed. The three men who made their escape were not seriously injured.

Nine workers for the Consolidation Coal Company at Van Lear were trapped behind a cave-in following an explosion at the Number Five Mine early Wednesday morning, apparently caused by gas. The accident occurred at 9 o'clock and rescue crews immediately began working to remove the men.

Those who were trapped behind the explosion were William Kretzer, Charles Kretzer, James Vaughan, John Gould, Deerwood Litz, Roy Murray, Virgil Clay, Frank Tuzzy and Sherley Hefford. Although everything was done to help the men, little hope for their survival was held.

The mine was not running that day and these men were in a worked-out section removing track. Little can be told until an investigation is held just what caused the explosion. They had gone into the mine earlier in the morning and had begun work. Three others who were working in the vicinity were far enough away to escape imprisonment and death.

As soon as the accident was reported, rescue units and safety squads arrived from every coal operation in this section of the state, one coming from as far away as Norton, Va. State Mine Department squads also reported and the work was under the supervision of John F. Daniel. Even the office force of the Consolidation

Coal Company was pressed into service and every modern means was used in the effort to help the men.

Large crowds of friends, relatives and spectators were on the scene of the accident as soon as it was reported and it was necessary to have special officers to keep them behind safety lines. Press services and news reel representative were on the scene attempting to get a full report of the tragedy early in the day.

As the Herald is going to press, it is reported that all of them have been removed from the mine, but little definite information could be learned. The first two bodies were taken from the scene of the accident early Thursday morning.

An arrest was made regarding the above-mentioned accident.

August 1, 1935—John F. Daniel, Chief of the State Department of Mines and Minerals is under bond of $10,000 on a charge of murder after he waived examining trial before County Judge H. B. Conley in Paintsville Tuesday. He had been arrested in Van Lear Monday on a warrant sworn out by John Mollett of Van Lear. The warrant charged him with murder and failure to do his duty at the mines at Van Lear. The charge arose out of the explosion which took the lives of nine miners at the Van Lear Mine Number Five on Wednesday, July 17.

Mr. Daniel was held in the Johnson County jail from Monday about noon until Tuesday morning at 10 o'clock when the examining trial was called by Judge Conley. He failed to make bond earlier because of the murder charge, which under the Kentucky law, prohibits bail on a murder charge until after the examining trial is held.

At the examining trial Tuesday morning, Mr. Daniel, through his attorneys Z. Wells and Clifford Pace, waived examination and his bond was set at $10,000. He made bond immediately with prominent local men as surety. He went immediately to Van Lear where he completed his business and then left for his headquarters in Lexington.

Mr. Mollett, in a statement to the Associated Press, said that he was convinced that the explosion was due to the negligence of Mr. Daniel and that he swore out the warrant entirely on his own responsibility so that the matter would have a thorough investigation. He said that Mr. Daniel had been requested to place more fire bosses in this mine but that he took no action on the matter. Mr. Mollett also said that he intended to prove at the trial in Circuit Court in November that Mr. Daniel was guilty of neglect of his duty.

The case will be presented to the Johnson County Grand Jury when it meets the first Monday in November. It is probable that the case will be called for trial during that term of court.

Interesting features are held at a community affair.

August 15, 1935—Playground activities at Van Lear are in full swing and last Friday night the girls of the community held a doll show.

A pet show was well attended and many entries were made, including dogs, cats, a bantam and a pigeon. A committee of judges consisting of John Spears, James Dodds and Charles Jasper found their job a difficult one, but after one dog fight was stopped and all the pets presented in an orderly way, awards were made.

First prize for puppies was awarded to Homer Preston, six years old, and Eddie Wills, five years old. Second prize went to Minnie Bell Cyrus, age 14, for cat entry. It is possible that a poultry show will be held by the children and an airplane exhibit.

Daily attendance runs from 100 to 125 children and adults and many kinds of recreation are enjoyed. Volley ball, soft ball, horseshoe pitching, swings, teeter-totters and sand boxes are included in three sessions daily. Scrap book making, storytelling, singing and free games also have their place on the daily program.

Special features have included a picnic, candy hunt, and chewing gum hunt and talent night. Each Friday night is Community Night with a special feature program differing each week. Daily playground hours are 9 to 11 a.m., 3 to 4 p.m. and 6:30 TO 8 P.M. Miss Marion Lynn is chairman of the Playground Committee and Mrs. Clyde P. Findlay is playground director.

The general promotion of the program was brought about by the Consolidation Coal Company and the cooperation by the various department heads. The program will be continued until school opens when the equipment will be used by the school children.

The Van Lear Boy Scouts were an active group.

August 15, 1935—Every boy in Van Lear has the opportunity to become a Boy Scout in a troop near his home as a result of organization work completed recently. B. M. Rogers, vice-president of the Area Scout Council and Horace Williamson, scout executive, conducted the work of organizing district committee.

Troops under the various scoutmasters meet on the following nights: Scoutmaster Junior Sparks meets his troop on Mondays, 6 p.m. at the Community Hall; Scoutmaster James Dodds meets his troop on Tuesdays at 6:30 p.m. at the Community Church; Scoutmaster John Spears meets his troop at 6:30 p. m. on Thursdays in the hotel at No. 155 Mine.

The membership is open to all boys who have reached their twelfth birthday and several boys from Auxier and West Van Lear have also applied for membership in the troops. When school starts, it is planned to conduct a boy-life survey through the schools and to continue a scoutmaster's training course.

Only seven boys attended the council camp near Whitesburg as each boy pays his own expenses. Next year it is hoped by the Scout leaders to have every boy in camp. A recent benefit show netted the troops a small treasury to be used for handbooks, badges, etc. Another benefit show is planned for the near future, at which time the Scouts will give a demonstration of Scout craft.

The District Committee has the following chairmen: Frank Price, local chairman; Frank Harris, vice-chairman; W. J. Brown, finance chairman; B.W. Hunter, court of honor chairman; Jess Holland, chairman leadership training; John Mollete, chairman troop organization; Dr. L. B. Wolfe, camping chairman; L. M. Griffin, civic chairman; and Clyde P. Findlay, district commissioner.

All troops were represented on a recent hike when a number of outdoor tests were passed and a campfire program closed the evening. Boys interested in becoming Scouts may see any of the above mentioned scoutmasters according to information furnished by the committee.

And the 1935 Van Lear Bank Mules' football season was well under way.

October 3, 1935—There are twenty-four men working hard for their respective positions. Much interest is manifested in the football team. Dr. Sheppard initiated a solicitation which has, to date, netted the football team $100. An order has gone in for new equipment and the Bank Mules should be able to "strut" in their new regalia of red hot jerseys, shoulder pads and shoes.

So far, the Bank Mules have won the following games: Kermit, West Virginia, 13-0; Louisa, 6-0; Martin 28-0; The schedule remains as follows: Belfry, Oct. 5, here: Pikeville, Oct. 12, there; Ft. Gay, Oct.19, here; Oct. 26, open; Paintsville, Nov. 2, here; Prestonsburg, Nov. 9, there; Jenkins, Nov. 16, here.

The football team and coach express their sincere appreciation for the backing given them this season. At a later date, it is hoped to publish names of those who have given financial support to the team.

Mine inspector freed on charge of murder.

November 12, 1935—John F. Daniel, chief inspector of mines in Kentucky, was given a full and free pardon last week by Governor Ruby Laffoon. He had been arrested and held under bond in Johnson County charged with murder and neglect of his duty in the death of nine miners at Van Lear when they were killed in an explosion there on July 17.

Mr. Daniel, served with a warrant sworn out by John Mollett, was arrested and lodged in the Johnson County jail without bond on the charge. He spent a night in jail awaiting the examining trial. His appearance bond was signed by some of the most outstanding citizens in Eastern Kentucky.

His case was to be heard by the members of the grand jury during this term of court. Much interest was shown in the case. As a result of the explosion in July, nine miners met their deaths. Those who were trapped and lost their lives were William Kretzer, Frank Tuzzy, Deerwood Litz, James Vaughan, Virgil Clay, Roy Murray, Charles Kretzer, L. S. Hereford and John Gool, all of Van Lear.

Governor Laffoon in issuing the pardon stated that he was convinced that Mr. Daniel was in no way responsible for the deaths of the nine miners.

Every effort was made to save them and safety crews from every coal operation in Eastern Kentucky were on hand in an attempt to rescue the trapped men.

A Van Lear miner was shot and killed at West Van Lear.

May 14, 1936—Worth Bayes, age about 25, was shot an almost instantly killed at West Van Lear last Saturday night at 8:00 o'clock. Glen Blevins, age about 35, is being sought by officers charged with the killing. Both men were residents of West Van Lear.

Bayes was a son of Leander Bayes and worked at Van Lear as a miner for a number of years. Blevins is a son of John E. Blevins. Both men are married and have families.

In the absence of evidence, a definite statement as to the shooting cannot be made, but the trouble between the two men is the aftermath of an old grudge and bad feeling which has existed between the two families for several years.

About eight years ago, Glen Blevins shot and killed Shug Bayes, a brother of Worth Bayes in thirty feet of the same spot where Worth Bayes was killed Saturday night. Blevins was tried and convicted and sentenced to 21 years in the penitentiary, but was pardoned after serving seven years of the term.

There were four witnesses to the shooting, it is said. At an inquest held before magistrate Claude Buckingham Sunday morning, it was brought out that Bayes and a companion were sitting on the railroad track about dark Saturday evening when Blevins came along and the shooting took place. During an exchange of shots between the two men, Bayes was mortally wounded. Blevins is said to have used a sawed-off shotgun, one of the loads taking effect in Bayes' breast near the heart. Bayes is said to have emptied his pistol at Blevins. One report says that Blevins was wounded and left a trail of blood as he fled from the scene.

A 44 year-old miner killed in the mines.

August 27, 1936—Frank (Ted) Anderson, age 44, was killed instantly in the mines at Van Lear last Saturday morning.

Mr. Anderson had worked as a miner at Van Lear for several years and was well known throughout this section.

On the day of the accident, he was working extra as a motorman. Two motors, it is reported, met head on going at full speed. The motor on which Anderson was riding was the lighter of the two and when the collision occurred, he was hurled beneath the wheels of the heavier motor and his body practically severed .When the body was picked up, it is reported, only a small sliver of skin held the body together.

Mr. Anderson was a nephew of George Anderson of Van Lear and Grant Anderson of Paintsville.

The body was preparing for burial by the undertaking department of the Paintsville Furniture Co. and taken to Salyersville where funeral services were held at the Missionary Baptist Church in charge of Rev. Caudill and Rev. Ghose.

Burial was in Blue Grass Cemetery beside his father, who preceded him in death many years ago.

Besides an aged mother who resides in Magoffin County, he is survived by one brother and several half brothers and sisters.

An Ohio woman whose husband had been working in the mines apparently killed herself in a gruesome and public way.

October 1, 1936—Mrs. John Campbell, age 32, of Van Lear, was instantly killed Sunday afternoon when she jumped from a taxi cab on the Mayo Trail about two and a half miles from Paintsville. Her death resulted from concussion of the brain from a fracture at the base of her skull.

According to Cecil Prater, driver of the cab, he was driving toward Paintsville with Mr. and Mrs. Campbell in the rear seat of his car. When the cab was about 200 yards north of the intersection of the Trail and the Garrett Highway, Mrs. Campbell suddenly jumped, flung open the door of the cab and leaped to the road. The motion of the car caused her to be thrown to the road with such violence the head was crushed.

An ambulance was called immediately and coroner O. E. Johnson rushed to the scene of the tragedy. She was brought to Paintsville and an inquest held Monday morning. The coroner's jury found that she came to her death by suicide.

She formerly lived in Ohio and the body was taken to Ironton Monday afternoon and burial was in that city Tuesday. She is survived by her husband, who has been working at Van Lear, and one daughter, who is 13 years old.

Another Van Lear man throws his hat into the political ring.

April 20, 1937—In its regular place in this issue of the Herald will be found the announcement of Guy Conley, of Van Lear, as a candidate for County Court Clerk of Johnson County. Mr. Conley is a young Republican of ability and would make an excellent official.

He is a member of a large family and is related to practically all the Conleys of this county. He is the son of Green Conley who served for many years as a member of the Van Lear police force.

Mr. Conley said this week that he intended to make an intensive campaign for the nomination.

In the fall of 1937, school bells rang again for the boys and girls of Van Lear.

September 2, 1937—Van Lear schools will open Tuesday, Sept. 7. A large enrollment is expected this year. An extra teacher and librarian have been employed in order to offer all the advantages possible in a modern twelve-grade system. Van Lear schools have a high rating and a well-trained teaching staff has been employed to maintain this standard. Van Lear patrons always show much interest in the schools and their programs. With these favorable circumstances, and a corps of teachers willing to work, a successful year is predicted.

The following teachers have been employed: Virgil Preston, principal; Brooksie Webb, sixth grade; Ethel Anderson, fifth grade; Mrs. Chas. E. Hall, fourth grade; Ollie Musick, third grade; Sola Philips, second grade; Mrs. O. L. Risner, first grade.

No. 5 School, Ben Short, principal; Francis Conley, third and fourth grades; Mrs. Verne P. Horne, first and second.

High School teachers include Vaughan LeMaster, principal; Mrs. L. Sheppard; Ruth Brown; Elizabeth Ladd; Mary Rice, librarian; Mrs. Alka Gibson; Hargus Isom, Coach; Bess Harris, attendance officer; Verne P. Horne, superintendent.

A former Van Lear miner passes.

September 16, 1937—Ed Cecil, 54, formerly for many years employed at Van Lear by the Consolidation Coal Company, died Saturday afternoon at the Paintsville Hospital. He had been living at Garrett for several years where he was employed as mine foreman for the Elkhorn Coal Corporation.

116

Mr. Cecil came to Johnson County from Ohio a good many years ago and was at one time employed by the Northeast Coal Company at Thealka.

The Paintsville Furniture Company's undertaking department took the body to Garrett where it remained in the home over night. Then the body was removed to Wellston, Ohio for burial Tuesday in the family cemetery there.

Mr. Cecil is survived by his wife and a brother, Oscar Cecil. The latter lives at Van Lear.

The Van Lear Order of the Eastern Star, a fraternal organization related to Freemasonry, installed officers.

October 14, 1937—A called meeting of the Order of the Eastern Star was held September 28 for installing officers for the year.

W. A. Gose of Kermit, W. Va., was installing officer. Mrs. Maggie Mollette was Marshall during the ceremonies.

The following new officers were installed—Mrs. Flossie Culbertson, Worthy Matron; F. C. Cunningham, Worthy Patron; Mrs. Anna Cunningham, Associate Matron; Vern P. Horne, Associate Patron; Mrs. Nettie Phillips, Secretary; Mrs. Ida Castle, Treasurer; Mrs. Maggie Mollette, Conductress; Miss Sola Phillips, Associate Conductress; Mrs. Thelma Williams, Chaplin; Mrs. Anna M. May, Marshall; and Mrs. Oscar Cecil, Organist.

Those appointed for the Star points were Mrs. Jewell Horne, Mrs. Irene Ditty, Mrs. Marshia Adams, Mrs. Emma Pinkerton, and Mrs. Pearl O'Bryan.

Those re-elected were Mrs. Hattie Adams, Warden, and John Pinkerton, Sentinel. At the close of the meeting, refreshments were served.

In 1937, there was another suicide.

October 28, 1937—Harry Fisher, age 45, prominent citizen of Van Lear, shot and killed himself at his home Sunday night. Mr. Fisher went into the bathroom and fired a load from an automatic shotgun into his body. Death was almost instantaneous.

The cause of Mr. Fisher's rash act is not known, but it is believed that despondency over home affairs was responsible for the deed.

Mr. and Mrs. Fisher were born in Pennsylvania but came to Van Lear twenty-four years ago where Mr. Fisher has been connected with the Consolidation Coal Company working in various capacities. At the time of his death, he was tipple foreman for the company and was paid a good salary. Money matters were evidently not the cause of his taking his own life.

It is said that Mr. Fisher called his youngest son, Harry Edward, 13, into his room and intimated the course he expected to take. He had made a will naming his youngest son as the sole beneficiary. The elder Fisher, it is said, is heir to considerable real estate in his old home in Pennsylvania. The death of Mr. Fisher was a shock to the citizens of Van Lear.

Funeral services were held at 3:30 Wednesday afternoon at the Van Lear M. E. Church, and were in charge of Reverend Everman, the pastor. Burial followed in the J. B. Wells Cemetery in Bridgeford Addition.

The Paintsville Furniture Company prepared the body for burial.

Mr. Fisher is survived by his wife and three daughters, Mrs. "Slim" Rose, Williamson, W.Va., Mrs. Douglas Smith and Miss Annebelle Fisher of Van Lear; two sons, James and Harry Edward at home.

Someone in the community decided to act as social correspondent.

October 28, 1937—Rev. Scaff is holding a revival at Van Lear.

Mr. and Mrs. Russell Sammons moved to a new home at Buffalo Monday.

Everybody is busy this week digging sweet potatoes.

Evelyn and Janet Selvage had as their guest Saturday night, Willard Selvage, George Ernest Robinson, Charles Burke and Mearl Smith.

Miss Virginia and Red Harmon attended a show at Van Lear Saturday night.

Sophia Conley attended a party at Paintsville Saturday night.

Mrs. Mearl Meade has returned to her home from Chicago. She has been visiting relatives there.

Mr. and Mrs. Bill Payne and son are moving to Allen Wednesday. They have been engaged in taking pictures at Van Lear for several weeks.

Several boys and girls of this place attended a party at Little Paint given in honor of Miss Helen Harmon.

Mary Francis Fairchild had a birthday party Saturday night. Several attended.

Irene Spears attended the ball game at Fleming Saturday.

United Mine Workers members from Van Lear and Thealka held a big parade in Paintsville.

April 7, 1938—Members of the United Mine Workers of America from Van Lear and Thealka locals, held a parade and meeting in Paintsville last Friday and heard a number of speeches by union officials.

The parade came into Paintsville through Euclid Avenue and Main Street after forming in Bridgford. The parade route was west on Main Street to Church Street, north on Church Street to Second Street, then west on Second Street to College and south to Main where they turned east again and stopped in the court house square.

Several speeches were made by various representatives of the union. E. L. Baker, of Pike County, spoke first and was followed by Paul Kellogg of Louisville; John Meade, president of Van Lear Local, United Mine Workers of America, was next, followed by W.J. Ward. John Marshall, former Jailer of Johnson

County, introduced the speakers and later made a short talk before the meeting ended.

The crowd was one of the most orderly ever seen here and citizens of Paintsville were pleased to have their neighbors pay a visit.

A Van Lear miner was near death after an altercation with another Van Lear man.

June 2, 1938—John Lominsky, a miner of Van Lear, is in the Paintsville Hospital in a dying condition as a result of cuts received in an altercation at Van Lear Sunday night. Earl Littlejohn, also of Van Lear, is being held in the Johnson County jail charged with cutting with intent to kill.

According to reports, an altercation arose between the two men over a debt, and Lominsky was slashed several times with a razor. Most serious of the cuts is a fourteen inch gash in his lower abdomen. As the *Herald* goes to press, little hopes are being held for his recovery.

Littlejohn was brought to the Johnson County jail soon after the cutting, and Wednesday night a warrant was issued for his wife who is charged with aiding and abetting.

Lominsky is a native of Poland and has been living in Van Lear for about 21 years. He is a naturalized citizen of the United States. No bond has been set for Littlejohn.

Then a week later, this story ran.

June 9, 1938—John Lominsky, 44, a miner for the Consolidation Coal Company at Van Lear, died at the Paintsville Hospital last Thursday night, June 2, as a result of cuts which he had received the preceding Sunday, Funeral services were held June 5, at the Van Lear Catholic Church. The Rev. Father Metzler officiated.

He is survived by his widow and two sons and two daughters. A brother, who lives in Pennsylvania, also survives. Mr. Lominsky was born in a small town in Poland and came to the United States in 1912. For more than 21 years he had lived in Van Lear where he had a wide circle of friends. He was a citizen of the United States, having received his naturalization papers many years ago.

He was cut several times in an altercation at Van Lear Sunday night, May 29. He was rushed to the Paintsville Hospital where physicians held little hope for his recovery from the first.

Earl Littlejohn, also of Van Lear, is being held in the Johnson County jail charged with inflicting the wounds which caused Lominsky's death. Mrs. Littleton, his wife, who is charged with aiding and abetting, was released on bond of $1,000.

County Judge Claude Buckingham has set Littlejohn's examining trial for Saturday of this week.

Coverage continued on the killing of John Lominsky.

June 16, 1938—Earl Littlejohn, a Van Lear miner charged Monday by the Johnson County Grand Jury with willful murder of John Lominsky, 44, also a miner for the Consolidation Coal Company at Van Lear, Tuesday was free on bond of $5,000.

His trial was set for Tuesday, June 28.

Bondsmen for Littlejohn were John Spears, Lon Davis, State Representative John B. Mollette; Fred Wetzel; Former State Representative, Frank Harris; William Harrison, Cal Moore, C. Littlejohn, father of the defendant, and his attorney, H. H. Ramey.

Lominsky, who came to the United States from Poland in 1912, died in the Paintsville Hospital June 2, after having been cut in an altercation the Sunday before.

An examining trial was held by County Judge Claude Buckingham Saturday at which Littlejohn was held for the grand jury action.

Littlejohn received two years in the penitentiary, according to the headline in the paper.

June 30, 1938—The case of Earl Littlejohn indicted for the slaying of John Lominsky at Van Lear on May 29, was called for trial Wednesday. Both Littlejohn and Lominsky were miners and had worked for the Consolidation Coal Company for several years past. Much interest was manifested in this trial and the court room was packed. Proof showed that the two men became engaged in a fist fight and during the fight Lominsky was cut in several places with a razor. Lominsky was disemboweled by a cut across the lower part of the abdomen. He died in the Paintsville Hospital the next day after the cutting.

Attorney Fred Meade acted as Commonwealth's Attorney pro tem and was assisted in the prosecution by Wheeler and Wheeler. Attorneys C. F. Pace of Paintsville, Harry Ramey and Walter Prater of Salyersville, represented the defense.

Later that summer, 10 Van Lear men took mine foremen exams.

August 11, 1938—Nine Van Lear men who took the examination at Lexington Saturday, July 30, for mine foremen, received first class papers entitling them to positions as foreman in the Consolidation Coal Company mines at Van Lear, according to an announcement from the office of John Daniel, State Mine Inspector.

Ten men took the examination and nine of them passed with high averages while only one failed to get first class papers which are required at the Van Lear mines because of the presence of gas in these mines.

Those who took the examination were Warren Auxier, Arthur McCourt, George Varner, Don Preston, Burdette Kretzer, John McClellan, Robert Conley, Earl Ditty, Everett "Dodge" Blevins and W. M. Dixon.

Verne Horne, principal of the Van Lear schools, went to Lexington with the men, taking part of them in his car, and assisted them in whatever way he could.

That same issue of the Herald *also had the following "society news."*

August 11, 1938—Mrs. Ed Castle has been very ill for the past few days but is improving slowly.

Mr. and Mrs. Clyde O'Bryan have as their guest Miss Freda Castle of Fallsburg, Ky.

The Sunday guests of Mr. and Mrs. Bascom Stanley were Miss Rachel Meddings and Jim Doulas Meddings of Van Lear.

Miss Betty Jean O'Bryan had as her guest Tuesday afternoon Gwendolyn Joe Layne of Paintsville.

Mrs. John B. Mollette, and little daughter Ann, were calling on Mr. and Mrs. Ed Castle Tuesday.

Miss Glenna Mae Campbell has returned home from Scranton, Ohio, where she was visiting her aunt, Mrs. Charles Roach.

Miss Betty Lambert, of Jenkins, is visiting her sister, Mrs. Virginia Daniel.

Another tragic accident was reported in December of 1938.

December 8, 1938—Roy Lee, age 34, was killed instantly in the mines of the Consolidation Coal Company at Van Lear Friday. His body was crushed and broken by a fall of slate in the room where he was working.

Mr. Lee was married and is survived by his wife and three children.

Ill luck seems to dog the footsteps of the Lee family. A few years ago his father committed suicide by firing a load from a shot gun into his head. Last year a brother of Roy Lee was killed in a mine accident.

Funeral services were held at the Van Lear M. E. Church Monday in charge of Rev. Mose Kitchen. Burial at Van Lear.

Besides his widow and three children the deceased is survived by his mother, Mrs. Ed Lee and a number of brothers and sisters.

A picture of the Van Lear High School basketball team ran under the headline "Van Lear Hoping for Better Times."

March 2, 1939—Van Lear High School fans were hoping for better times come next basketball season. The team has a fair record, but as there are no seniors and only one junior on the squad, the fans are expecting a big improvement next season. The team, from the left, crouching, Junior Clifton, Willard Wells, Clyde Groves, Mason Castle and Billy Cassel. Standing, Esmer Williams, Ty Wallace and Coach B. Preston.

Trouble at the mines required a hearing by the arbitration board.

March 23, 1939—Labor trouble which has kept mines of the Consolidation Coal Company at Van Lear closed for a month may be settled in a few days.

A case covering the situation has been filed by the company with the Board of Arbitration and a hearing was set for yesterday at Ashland. Hearing of the case was postponed when it was learned that Sam Cady, president of District 30, United Mine Workers, would not leave the wage conference now in session in New York.

An official of the company said yesterday that it was ready to "meet any time and at any place to decide the issues in this case." He also said that the company would insist on an early hearing.

It is the opinion that a date will be set for the coming week.

On the day the mines ceased operations, there were 692 men on the payroll.

Miners, operators and the general public are hopeful that this trouble will be ended in a short while so that the men who have been idle may return to their jobs. Since the mine has been closed the workers have lost more than $100,000 and this has been reflected in the general business activity of the entire country.

May 25, 1939—The Northeast Coal Company, Auxier, is working with practically a full crew, and the Consolidation Coal Company at Van Lear has returned about three hundred men to the payroll. No work has yet been done at Thealka. It is understood that the Millers Creek Coal Company will begin operations in a few days. This mine has been closed since early in February, and the Van Lear operation has been closed since February 14.

A Van Lear youth takes first honors at state fair.

September 21, 1939—In the annual 4-H poultry judging contest at the Kentucky State Fair September

11-15, Vencil Young, of the Van Lear 4-H Club, placed first in the state. Twenty-eight teams from various sections of the state competed in this contest. Vencil scored 437 points out of a possible 500. This is twice in the last three years that Jonson County has had the prize winner in the state contest. Hobart Wells, of the Williamsport club, winning first place in 1937.

This year's team was composed of Vencil Young, of Van Lear Club; Henry Wells, of Odds Club; Ochell Preston, of the Thelma Club, and Junior McCloud, of the West Van Lear Club. They won third place in the state contest, with Breathitt County ranking first and Morgan second.

Total premiums won by the team amounted to $19.00.

A Van Lear miner died shortly after going to work.

September 28, 1939—Ed Castle, an employee of the Consolidation Coal Company, at Van Lear, died suddenly shortly after entering the mines Monday afternoon. Mr. Castle had been in his usual good health and had worked during the morning shift. Shortly after entering the mine during the afternoon shift, he became ill and was brought to the outside where he died within a few minutes. The exact cause of his death is unknown.

Mr. Castle had resided at Van Lear for several years and was prominent in social and lodge circles. He was a member of Van Lear Lodge No. 885, F. & A. M., an Odd Fellow, and a member of the Junior Order United

American Mechanics. He served two years as a member of the Van Lear police force.

Mr. Castle was 55 years of age, having been born March 23, 1884.

Funeral services were held at 10 a. m. at the Van Lear M. E. Church. The body was then taken to Garred Chapel in Lawrence County, where short services were also held. Burial followed in the Wilson Cemetery three miles south of Louisa.

Mr. Castle had no children. Besides his widow, Mrs. Ida Wilson Castle, he is survived by two brothers and three sisters, Harry and Walter Castle, Mrs. Julia Bowe, Mrs. Nevada Cochran, and Mrs. Lou Abshire.

Chapter Four: 1940-1947

*T*he decade of the 1940s was a double whammy for Van Lear residents. Just as it did for every town across America, World War II devastated the little Johnson County town. Then soon after the boys came home, the Consolidation Coal Company divested its interests in Millers Creek Coal and a group of businessmen from Pikeville paid $300,000 for the town. Soon after that, Van Lear residents who lived in "company houses" were told to either buy their homes or be evicted.

But despite the changes this particular decade wrought upon Van Lear's citizens, many newspaper articles during the last eight years covered in this chapter (1940-1947) regarded many positive and normal events. A high school field trip, the election of officers for the Van Lear Woman's Club, and a story of heroism in the mines were featured during the forties in The Paintsville Herald.

Unfortunately, there was also bad news. Three mining fatalities, one report of a Van Lear man being killed in the war, and two more homicides were also reported.

The decade of the 1940s began with the report of the death of an elderly man.

February 15, 1940—Bailey Bowling, possibly the oldest citizen of Johnson County, died at the home of a son at Van Lear Wednesday of this week. According to his children, he was 103 years old, having been born in the year 1837.

Mr. Bowling was a Virginian and came to the Big Sandy Valley with his parents when a child. He had been in good health until a week before his death.

His aged wife died seven months ago. She, too, was near the century mark.

The aged man was the father of 15 children, 13 of whom survives. Those living are P. A. Bowling, Johns Creek; Joe Bowling, Van Lear; John Bowling, Mance Bowling and Amos Bowling, Beaver Creek; Lige Bowling, Pike County; Boyd Bowling, W. Va.; Mrs. Fan Pendleton and Mrs. Rissie Dawson, Daniels Creek; Mrs. Paulina Blair, and Mrs. Clarinda Ward, Johns Creek, and Mrs. Nancy Kessenger, of Paintsville.

Funeral and burial took place at Van Lear in charge of the Preston Funeral Home.

Van Lear High School students visited Paintsville.

February 15, 1940—The freshman class of the Van Lear High School was in Paintsville Friday on a tour of inspection of the various business establishments of the city. Verne P. Horne, principal of the school, was in charge of the students.

The class visited the *Herald* office and was shown a newspaper plant in operation and the process of printing. The students were impressed after being shown through the plant.

The students who visited here Friday were Nellie Sparks, Richard Adams, Ann Beers, Betty Jean Brickley, Arnold Blanton, Jimmie Stanley, James Vaughan, Chester Gaiskl, Tony Clifton, June Rowlette, Ronena Isaac, Lucille Daniel and Bertha Kretzer.

Also, Josephine Kretzer, Ilene Lewis, Leonard Meade, Albert Murphy, George Varner, Layton Hughes, Doris Ann Bevins, Laura Phelps, Hondel Adams, Lois Thomas, Curtis Collins, Eula Pelphrey, Earl Williams, Marcus Spears, Charles Bowling, Neva Jean Selvage, Maxine Sellards, Oral Trimble, and John Marshall.

The Van Lear Woman's Club elected officers and named delegates to attend the convention.

April 18, 1940—The Woman's Club of Van Lear met at the Club House Thursday evening, April 11, at 7:30 p.m. with Mrs. C. P. Shields and Mrs. Hansford Teater as joint hostesses.

The meeting was called to order by the president, Mrs. C. P. Shields. Minutes of the last meeting were given by Mrs. J. R. McKinney, secretary. During the business session delegates were nominated to attend the Woman's Club Convention to be held at Louisville

May 8, 9 and 10. Mrs. C. P. Shields and Mrs. J. R. McKinney were chosen for delegates and Mrs. Bob Blake and Mrs. Homer Shearer were elected as alternates.

New officers elected for the next year were Mrs. C. P. Shields, president; Mrs. Arlo Wallace, vice president; Mrs. J. R. McKinney, secretary; and Mrs. Paul Wetzel, treasurer.

The club is sponsoring the picture "Abe Lincoln in Illinois," at the Van Lear Theatre Thursday and Friday, April 18 and 19. The money is to be used in sending delegates to the convention.

The benefit bridge party given by the club is to be held at the Club House Saturday evening, beginning at 7:30 p. m.

More society news was passed on to the Herald for publication.

April 18, 1940—After a few days of very cold weather, we are glad to see the sun shine again.

L. Baldridge, of Sciotoville, Ohio, has been holding services in Van Lear.

Mrs. Flem Conley, who has been sick, is some better.

Charlie Castle, from Paintsville, was calling on friends Sunday, in Van Lear.

Samuel Colvin, Bob Auxier and Chester Auxier, Manila, were calling on Verna Castle at Van Lear, Saturday.

An old-time square dance was given at the Van Lear gym Saturday night. Music by the Van Lear Jug Band. Everybody reported a good time.

Everyone at this place is busy with garden work.

Mrs. Julia McNeer, of East Point and Mrs. Tom Colvin, of this place were in Paintsville on business Saturday.

Little Miss Frances Castle, of Paintsville, is visiting her grandparents at Van Lear.

Johnnie Lambert, of Jenkins, was the Saturday night guest of Johnnie Colvin.

Another mine fatality was reported in early July.

July 4, 1940—Ben Hicks, age about 45, was instantly killed in the mines of the Consolidation Coal Company at 9:30 Monday morning.

He died instantly following a premature explosion of monobel with which he was shooting coal. No one knows just how the accident occurred as he was working alone at the time.

The body was badly mangled. Evidently he had the monobel in his hands as the main force of the blast hit him in the breast.

This is the first fatality to occur at the Van Lear mines for more than a year, Leslie Sword, another miner from Van Lear said here Monday.

Hicks is survived by a wife and one child.

Funeral services were held at Van Lear July 4.

A Van Lear man was badly injured in a slate fall.

October 10, 1940—A. B. Murray was injured in a slate fall in the mines of the Consolidation Coal Company at Van Lear at 5 o'clock Tuesday afternoon. Mr. Murray has been a machine man in the mines for fourteen years and with the company for fifteen years, residing at Van Lear.

He is suffering from a broken back.

The injured man was brought to the Paintsville Hospital where he is reported to be in a serious condition.

He would have finished his work for the shift within a short time when the accident happened.

Mr. Murray is a son of H. B. Murray, of the Flat Gap section at the county.

Politics once again began to appear in the pages of the Herald. *A Van Lear man, Guy Conley, ran the following announcement beneath his photo.*

March 13, 1941—I take this method of announcing myself as a candidate for the office of County Court Clerk subject to the action of the Republican Primary on Saturday, August 2, 1941.

I was born and have lived all my life in Johnson County. I am a descendant of some of the oldest and largest Johnson County families. I am the son of Green Conley and Molly Burke Conley who now live at Van Lear. My grandparents on my father's side were Hiram

Conley and Mary Anne Estep Conley; on my mother's side, they were Calvin and Martha Music Burke.

I am 30 years old. For the last six years of my life, I have been a church member and have lived a Christian life. I attended the Van Lear Elementary and High Schools, and have held responsible positions in the business world.

You know as well as I, of course, that the office of county court clerk is one of the most important of the county offices. It is there that all important transactions in the county are recorded as well as the proceedings of the County and Fiscal Courts. The issuance of various licenses and other duties of a clerical nature are performed by this office. It is important that these records should be kept accurately and that they be made available at a moment's notice to any citizen entitled to such information.

I understand the duties of the office. My education and business experience qualify me to perform these duties.

If elected, it will be my purpose to set a high mark for efficient service. While rendering efficient service I shall see that the public, and I mean every individual, is treated kindly and courteously. I believe that is what the people want in their public officials, efficient and courteous service. Anyway, that shall be my motto.

It is my belief that an elected official should be a humble servant of the people, not their boss.

I hope to be able to see each of you before the election. -- Guy Conley

Two Van Lear miners were awarded medals for extraordinary rescue work.

March 27, 1941—At approximately two o'clock on the afternoon of August 27, 1940, motorman Laud Webb and brakeman William Titlow were pulling empties in No. 7 south section of Mine 155, Consolidation Coal Company at Van Lear, Kentucky. When the switch was cleared, Titlow gave the stop signal, threw the switch and signaled the motorman to come back. At this time, Titlow and section foreman C. L. Risner, were standing at the switch hole. After Titlow gave the signal the trip did not move and both Titlow and Risner heard Webb groan.

The two men ran down to the motor, a distance of about ninety feet, and found Webb lying on the electric wire. They first tried to remove Webb by taking the trolley pole off the wire but this failed; they then got up on the rubber mat in the motor and with dry gloves pulled Webb clear of the wire and stretched him on the bottom of the clearance side of the track.

Although Webb was apparently dead, Titlow immediately began artificial respiration while Risner treated for shock. After about ten minutes continual giving of artificial respiration they noticed Webb draw a long breath. Risner then ran to the telephone and asked that a doctor be sent in. Risner returned to where Webb was and by this time he was partly revived and delirious. It took the two men to hold him down to prevent over-exertion. In about twenty minutes, Harry McCarty, section foreman on an adjoining section, came to the scene. In a very short time, Dr. Chas. McEwen arrived, examined Webb's condition, and gave him a certain treatment and he was then placed on a stretcher and taken outside; these men watching his breathing closely during the trip.

Dr. McEwen sent Webb to the hospital at Paintsville. Webb lost 82 days from work, received burns on the left elbow, right shoulder, right temple and head, in addition to serious shock.

The ability of these two men to administer artificial respiration and their coolness and efficiency in carrying out the difficult work of removing the man from contact with the electric wire and treating him without inflicting further injury, undoubtedly saved a life.

This matter was laid before the board of the National Safety Council and William Titlow was, on March 13, 1941, presented the National Safety Council President's Medal and Certificate for saving a human life. Also O. L. Risner was given the Council's Certificate of assistance in this act of rescue. [*Two different names were given in this story for Mr. Risner. At the beginning he was referred to as C. L. Risner. At the end of the story he was referred to as O. L. Risner.*]

When a play about an old-time school was shown at Van Lear, it became obvious that the cessation of mining work at Consolidation had no effect on school spirit.

April 21, 1941—A very unusual and entertaining program was given in the Van Lear High School by the members of the Parent-Teachers Association last

Tuesday evening. Since the coal mines discontinued operations April 1, some people might think that the miners and their wives would be more or less pessimistic and non-cooperative, but such is not the case. It is true that the miners would like to be at work, but they are not allowing the situation to prevent them from doing some good in the community.

One of the best programs ever given in Van Lear, and possibly as good for its kind, even in the state, was put on by the men and women in the Central School Association. The program was not only entertaining but timely and educational. It was indeed a credit to the community.

In order to show the advantages of our educational system over that of forty years ago, a mock school, under the able leadership of Frank Harris, who was a teacher at that time, was organized and carried out before a large audience. The school room of the period was depicted authentically. Old benches with recitation seats in front; a table with water bucket and cup. Even the texts used were old copies that had been preserved. The students were dressed for the occasion, too. Hair parted in the middle, hanging in plaits down the back with loud and large ribbons. Some barefooted, some with shoes of a coarse style. The subjects taught and the conversations were in keeping with the time.

Real talent in acting was displayed on this program which was carried out in minute detail. The persons taking part were Mrs. Sophie Lambert, Mrs. Homer Shearer, Eunice Salyer, Mrs. Homer Cunningham, Reese Michael and Ruby Dickerson.

Mrs. Lowell Phillips used the same group, dressed in modern fashion, to show how a modern school is taught. Mrs. Phillips did a splendid job with the modern version. Also a trio, Miss Margie Conley, Mr. Cavern and Mr. Guy Conley, sang some beautiful selections. This endeavor is one of which the entire community is proud.

And a Van Lear man joined the Navy.

October 2, 1941—Frank Campigotto, Jr., son of Mr. and Mrs. Frank Campigotto, of Van Lear, reported September 25, for active duty at the U. S. Naval Training Station at Great Lakes, Ill., where he began his career in the U.S. Navy. His first phase of Navy life will be a 6-week course in intensive training in primary seamanship and naval procedure at the training station.

On the morning of December 7, 1941, the Imperial Japanese Navy launched a surprise attack on the U.S. naval base at Pearl Harbor, Hawaii, an event that led to the United States' entry into World War II.

December 11, 1941—Elmer Hitchcock, 22, Van Lear, began his career in the U. S. Navy December 5, when he reported for duty at the U. S. Training Station at Great Lakes, Ill.

At the close of a six-week period of basic seamanship training, Hitchcock will be given a 10-day furlough. He then will report back at the station for assignment to active duty at sea or to one of the many naval technical schools.

With a war going on, Van Lear miners aided in war work.

January 15, 1942—The miners of Van Lear have shown their patriotism and demonstrated their sympathy with the government's movement to crush Japan and the Axis powers.

At their meeting of Local Union No. 5834, United Mine Workers of America, held at Van Lear Saturday, January 10, the miners voted to buy a $100 U.S. Defense Bond to be paid out of the treasury of the union, according to a statement this week by Ray Daniels, district supervisor of the organization who was present at the meeting.

At the same meeting, the miners voted to pay $100 a month each to the American Red Cross war fund. It is estimated by Mr. Daniels that the miners of Van Lear will pay into the treasury of the American Red Cross $600 or $700 per month.

As the United States' war efforts ramped up, Kentucky coal miners continued to dig deep for defense.

February 26, 1942—Sam Caddy, Lexington, president of District 30, United Mine Workers of America, has announced that allotments from the pay rolls of Kentucky coal miners for the purchase of defense bonds are increasing at the rate of "not less than $10,000 a day." On the basis of reports of 44 of the state's 99 U. M. W. A. local unions, miners are buying $308,285 worth of bonds each payday, Mr. Caddy stated. The U. M.W.A. Administrative staff, on each payday, is buying an additional $6,000 worth.

The local at Inland Steel Company at Wheelright is furnishing $87,000 for the purchase of bonds, the next highest being $83,400 allotted by the combined local unions of Consolidation's mines at Van Lear, Jenkins, Dunham, and McRoberts. Payroll allotments at other mines range from $200 to $29,700.

Figures on the locals at Van Lear and Northeast Mines are not complete. The work is just getting started but from preliminary reports, Johnson County's miners will rank among the top in buying defense bonds.

The war overshadowed every facet of life on the home front.

November 12, 1942—To the boys from Van Lear in the service of Uncle Sam: Especially Arlie McCallister, who is stationed in Alaska and had a poem in *The Herald* asking for more Van Lear news.

The whole community is back of you boys and knows we wouldn't be having the freedom and peace we are enjoying if it were not for you boys; so we are trying to do our part by buying defense bonds with 10 percent of our earnings that you may be the best equipped army in the world. Keep the good work going and we will try to keep the news coming each week.

Mrs. Hershell McCallister is visiting her mother, Mrs. Frank Tootsy, of Kingwood, W. Va.

Miss Virginia Meddings and Miss Eloise Hall were the Saturday night guests of Miss Naomi Rucker.

Ralph Ward, U. S. Navy, stationed at Great Lakes, Ill., is visiting his parents, Mr. and Mrs. Asbury Ward.

Mr. and Mrs. John Spears and daughter Billie, were shopping in Huntington last week.

Miss Louise Brown, of Cincinnati, Ohio, was visiting her grandparents, Mr. and Mrs. B. L. Gibson.

Wayne Salyer and Elvin Pelphrey, of Galloway, Ohio, were visiting friends in Van Lear.

Gid Cyrus and Chester Picklesimer, returned home from the Army after being given a medical discharge.

Mr. and Mrs. Nick O'Breasly and family were visiting in Whitesburg last week.

Mrs. Willard Wells is visiting her parents, Mr. and Mrs. Fred Caudill. Mrs. Wells is now employed in Seattle, Wash.

Mr. and Mrs. John Sellards have moved to Paintsville.

Mrs. Emma See, of Louisa, was visiting her brother, Bill Fraley, Saturday.

Cpl. Scott Conley is visiting his parents, Mr. and Mrs. Green Conley. Cpl. Conley is stationed in Nevada. Mrs. Alex Farmer is visiting her sister, Mrs. Estill Daniel, of Xenia, Ohio.

Francis Lemaster, of Chandlersville, was the Sunday guest of Jack Fraley.

A revival meeting will begin at the Van Lear Mission November 15, with the Rev. Hattie Craft in charge.

Sgt. T. J. Banks, stationed at Camp Woods, Texas, was visiting relatives here Friday. He was accompanied by his brother Dingus Banks, of Prestonsburg.

Virgil Burchett and Harry McCarty were in Detroit last week.

Mr. and Mrs. Henry Conley and children, Anna Lou and Jim, of Ashland, were the weekend guests of relatives.

The Van Lear Woman's club held its regular meeting Friday night at the Club House. Those attending were Mrs. Pat Lambert, president; Mrs. Eddie Meade, Secretary, Mrs. Nick O'Breasley, Treasurer; Mrs. Ralph Salyer; Mrs. Earl Meade; Mrs. Walter Barker; Mrs. Jack Mathers, and her guest, Mrs. Clyde Arrowood.

Plans were made for a party to be given Friday, November 13, for Mrs. Carlos Goble, who was once a member of the Van Lear Woman's Club, but is now living at Jenkins were her husband is employed.

Early in the New Year, another Van Lear man lost his life in the mines.

February 4, 1943—A tragic accident occurred at Van Lear January 28, which resulted in the death of William Harrison Blevins of that neighborhood.

He and his father-in-law, Gayland Franklin, had gone to a country mine to secure coal for home consumption. After the men had been in the mine for some time a slate fall took place and Blevins was caught in the avalanche of slate. Franklin was struck but uninjured. He ran for help and six other men aided in extricating the body.

He was married to Miss Mary Franklin and the father of three children.

He was a member of a large family of thirteen children, and was a son of James A. Garfield Blevins and Nora Meade Blevins, who reside at West Van Lear. He was 28 years old, having been born July 5, 1915.

Besides his widow, he is survived by Chester and Lester Blevins, twins, and Gayland Blevins. He is also survived by his parents and the following brothers and sisters: James Blevins, Mrs. Fannie Wetzel, and Mrs. Mervie Hall, Paul, Mrs. Bertha Drake, George Beecher, Bridgett, Austria Faye, Richard, Odell, Myra and Helen.

Funeral was held at 10:00 Sunday morning at the home of his parents at Van Lear, Rev. Guy W. Preston, officiating.

He was member of the Christian Church at West Van Lear.

An argument over politics was said to be the cause of a shooting in which a Van Lear man was killed.

March 4, 1943—A special grand jury was impaneled today to investigate the shooting of Woodrow Sparks of Van Lear by Alonzo Daniel also of Van Lear Sunday night. Sparks, 28 years old, died instantly, the bullet entering his chest close to his heart.

It is reported that both men were riding in the car of Grant Hill. Richard Collins and R. W. Dennison, Jr. were also occupants of the car. Hill was driving and Dennison and Sparks were in the front seat with him, Dennison in the middle. Collins and Daniel were on the back seat. According to reports, Sparks and Daniel exchanged words in a political argument, Sparks turning around with his knees on the seat facing Daniel. It is reported that Daniel pulled out his 32-20 caliber pistol firing into Sparks' chest.

The men were riding in Bridgford at the time of the shooting. Daniel is said to have pointed his gun at the other men, demanding Hill to stop the car. When the car came to a halt, Daniel forced the men out of the car, getting out himself. Hill, Collins and Dennison fled toward Paintsville and Daniel ran toward Van Lear. The dead man was left in the car.

The men notified Paintsville police of the shooting. City Councilman Hannibal Wheeler drove the car with the victim beside him to the City Hall where Chief of Police W. B. Bailey took over driving to the Paintsville Furniture Undertaking establishment. There a coroner's inquest was held determining that Sparks was killed by a shot fired from Daniel's pistol.

Daniel was picked up a few hours after the killing at his son's home in Van Lear by Sheriff Lester Adams

.

That spring, the Van Lear School held a ceremony for the 25 students advancing to ninth grade.

May 13, 1943—The eighth grade graduation exercise for Van Lear School is scheduled for Wednesday night, May 19, at 8:30 P. M., in the Baptist Church. A very interesting program is being prepared for this occasion. All the boys and girls in the class are taking part in the program.

Listed below are the names of those that finish their grade school career: Betty Adams, Bonita Jo Burchwell, Betty Burnett, Arretta Cantrell, Ernestine Coleman and Betty Sue Hall.

Also, Opal Honeycutt, Dorothy June Pack, Lois Pettry, Lorene Picklesimer, Christina Satinkoff, Darlene Sparks, Meagan Waddell and Betty Webb. Also, Billie Jo Wells, Hope Young, Ruby Lee Borders, Paul Brickley, Charles Conley, Jr., Milburn Conley, Elmer Dawson, Johnny Gaiski, Jack Mather, Robert McCarty and Aulden Williamson.

The Van Lear Red Cross was working hard to help with the war effort.

July 29, 1943—7,737, 2 X 2 bandages have been made in the month of July. The quota was 14,000. With every woman doing her part the quota will be completed this week. Those working last week were Mrs. George Hall, who has made a perfect record of folding the largest number. Last week in seven hours, she folded eight hundred perfect bandages.

Mrs. Ruby Lee (Hall) Kitts, Washington, D. C., came to help and folded five hundred in seven hours. The others who worked were Mrs. Clyde Arrowood, Miss

Mildred Hicks, Miss Irene Castle, Miss Margaret Davis, Mrs. Lawrence Meddings, Mrs. Sam Phelps, Mrs. Harry Adams, Mrs. G. C. Chambers, Mrs. G. C. Stapleton, Mrs. Estill Lewis, Mrs. Ben Adams, Mrs. Norman Fraley and Miss Betty Brickley.

Total number of bandages last week was 2,612.

It is every woman's and girl's patriotic duty to come and help fold these bandages.

You will be helping your boys and yourselves.

The war news regarding Van Lear dominated the Herald.

May 4, 1944—Word has been received by Mrs. William Roy Lambert, Van Lear, that her husband Pvt. William Roy Lambert was wounded seriously in battle on Lose Negros Island, March 2.

Pvt. Lambert was a coal miner before he entered the service. He is 30 years old.

Many women also joined the service during the war.

July 13, 1944—Lt. Helen Meade, daughter of Mrs. Jeff Meade, Van Lear, is now serving in Italy. She is a graduate of Van Lear School and St. Elizabeth's Hospital of Covington, Kentucky, where she completed her nurse's training in 1940. Before enlisting in the army on October 10, 1942, she was a nurse at the Paintsville Hospital for two years. She was the first Johnson County nurse to volunteer for the army.

Overseas eleven months, Lt. Meade has been awarded a medal for being one of the first to set up the 118th Station Hospital and caring for the wounded boys in Italy.

A brother, Earl Meade, S 2/C, is stationed at Norfolk, Va.

Yet another fatality occurred in the Van Lear Mines.

July 20, 1944—In a tragic accident at Van Lear last Friday, John Gaiski, 62, one of the oldest employees of the Consolidation Coal Company's Van Lear mine, lost his life. Three other men, Canie Conley, Green Burke and Ganes Rice, who were working with Gaiski, were uninjured.

It is understood that the four men were pulling steel from a worked-out section of the mine when slate, said to be fifteen inches thick and sixty-seven feet long, fell. The three who escaped were reported to be at the front end of the car on which the steel was being loaded and jumped from under the falling slat. Gaiski, who it is said was at the back of the car, could not get out of the way in time. He died shortly after his arrival at the Paintsville Hospital where he was rushed after the accident.

The dead man had been a resident of Van Lear for thirty-two years. It is reported that Mr. Gaiski had intended to retire from his work within a short time.

A son, Walter, was killed in Italy in January of this year.

Surviving are his wife Frances and several children who were all present for the funeral services conducted Tuesday morning, with the exception of a daughter who was ill.

Rev. R. R. Rose officiated at the services. Burial was made in the cemetery by the side of his home under direction of the Jones Funeral Home.

Then came the report of another soldier being killed in the war....

August 17, 1944—Pfc. Onda Murphy, who entered the service November 3, 1942, was killed in action in France on D-Day, June 6. He was in the North African and Sicilian invasion with his buddy, Curtis Burchett, Stambaugh, who was also killed on June 6.

Pfc. Murphy was the son of Mr. and Mrs. Everett Murphy, of Van Lear. He attended Van Lear High School and was popular with his classmates. He was farming when he entered the service at age 26. A few weeks after joining the armed forces he underwent a serious operation at an army hospital in Georgia. He was shipped overseas early in 1943 without ever coming home on furlough.

Pfc. Murphy is survived by his four brothers, Albert, Lawrence, Herschel and Glen, all of Van Lear, and five sisters, Mrs. Frank Stambaugh, Mrs. Roy Brown, Myrtle, Josephine and Minerva Ellen, and grandfather George Powers of Mealy.

...and another miner killed on the job.

August 31, 1944—Charles Gool, 32, met almost instant death early Friday afternoon when two empty mine cars ran over him at the Consolidation Coal Company's Van Lear mine. Gool, a brakeman at the mine, either fell or jumped to switch cars. It is not known definitely just how the accident occurred, but it is understood that a number of empties were being switched back in the mines. When the accident occurred the two cars that passed over his body were derailed, and workmen rushed to the scene. A doctor was summoned at once. However, before his arrival and only a short time after the accident, Gool was pronounced dead.

The funeral was held Sunday at the Hager Hill Holiness Church with Rev. E. L. Baldridge of Sciotoville, Ohio, conducting the services. Due to the inclemency of the weather, interment was postponed until Monday morning when the body was laid to rest at the West Van Lear cemetery.

Mr. Gool was married to Esta McDowell. They have three sons. His foster father, John Gool, was killed in the Van Lear explosion in 1935.

Not all of the Van Lear news was tragic.

August 31, 1944—With the Ninth Infantry Division in France, Sergeant Delmer B. Williams, son of Mr. and Mrs. Houston Williams, of Van Lear, recently was decorated with the Silver Star by Major General Manton

S. Eddy, commanding general of the Ninth Infantry Division, for gallantry in action during Allied Operations in Normandy.

Sgt. Williams is a veteran of the invasion of French North Africa at Algiers and the Tunisian and Sicilian campaigns, and participated in the Ninth Division's spectacular dash across the Cherbourg Peninsula. The Ninth Division was the first to enter the port city of Cherbourg.

In addition to the Silver Star, Sgt. Williams wears the Combat Infantryman Badge, American Defense Medal, European African Mediterranean Campaign Ribbon with three Battle Stars.

A photo of a Van Lear sailor, along with a brief caption, appeared in the Herald.

November 30, 1944—Earl Meade S 1-c, is serving in Scotland. The son of Mrs. Jeff Meade of Van Lear enlisted in the Navy March 8, 1944 and was sent to the U. S. Naval Training at Sampson, New York, for special assignment. After Boot Training, he spent a brief furlough with his family, later being sent to Norfolk, Va., for more advanced training. He has been overseas since July. Seaman Meade has a sister, Lt. Helen Meade, with the Army Nurses Corps in Italy.

January 11, 1945—T-Sgt. Carl F. Castle, 23, nephew and foster son of Mr. and Mrs. James King, Van Lear, and husband of Mrs. Emma J. Castle, Martin, was killed in action in France December 14, according to a telegram sent to his wife by the War Department this week.

Son of Preston Castle and the late Mrs. Castle, Van Lear, Sgt. Castle was raised from a small child by his uncle and aunt Mr. and Mrs. Jim King.

Sgt. Castle entered service five years ago. He served in Iceland for a year, was returned to the United States, and then later was sent overseas last October. He attended the Van Lear schools.

On the home front, there was another tragedy.

February 8, 1945—Judith Malinda Marshall, 2½ - year-old daughter of Pvt. and Mrs. Thomas Marshall, Van Lear, died in a local hospital early Sunday morning a few minutes after being brought in for treatment of burns sustained shortly before. Her sister, Diana, 4, who was critically burned, is expected to recover.

It is understood that the children were in their home at Van Lear, and that the youngest caught fire from the open grate, Diana becoming burned when attempting to extinguish the flames.

Funeral services were held Tuesday at the Van Lear Baptist Church under the direction of the Jones Funeral Home. Burial was in the Wells cemetery. The father is serving in the army.

The children's grandparents are Mr. and Mrs. John Marshall, Wayland, and Mr. and Mrs. Howard Painter, Van Lear.

Consolidation, meanwhile, was recognized for its war efforts.

March 22, 1945—For outstanding service to the nation, the management and men at 114 bituminous coal mines and two anthracite collieries have been voted "Coal for Victory" awards, Coal Age, a McGraw-Hill publication announced today. The awards were offered by Coal Age, with the support and cooperation of the Solid Fuels Administration for War, to stimulate war production, foster mining progress and honor outstanding accomplishment. They are the first such awards ever offered the nation's coal industry.

Two awards were offered: the "War Production Efficiency" award and the ""Victory Coal Award," and mines or collieries could win either or both. Consolidation Company's Van Lear and Jenkins mines were awarded the "Victory Coal Production" award.

Twenty Van Lear High School seniors donned caps and gowns and received their diplomas in mid-May, 1945.

May 3, 1945—Baccalaureate services for Van Lear High School will be held at the Baptist Church Sunday, May 13 at 11:00.

Commencement exercises will be at the Baptist Church on May 17 at 8:00 p. m. J. L. Patton, director of Mayo State Vocational School, will deliver the address, and Hysel Burchett, principal, will present the graduating class diplomas. Seniors to graduate are Garnett Adams, Phyllis Barber, Peggy Beers, salutatorian, Doris Ann Burton, Clyde Archie Collins, Joyce Irene Collins, Hester Crum and James Hall.

Also, Joe Edgar Hewelett, Billie Ann Kelly, Louise King, valedictorian, June Lemaster, Audrey Grace Lewis, Bruce Phelps, Randy Rice, Audrey Setser, Lottie Setser, Illena Wells, Jack Williams and Betty Young.

A Van Lear man was shot and killed in August.

August 16, 1945—Willie Childs, colored, Van Lear, native of Birmingham, Ala., was shot and killed near his home in Wolf Pen Hollow on Sunday morning, August 12.

Lodie Baxter, colored, is being held in the Johnson County jail pending examining trial.

The inquest will be held on August 18.

That fall, Van Lear had a lively election.

November 8, 1945—Much enthusiasm was shown in Tuesday's election in the town of Van Lear. Farris Arrowood was elected Police Judge with a majority of 10 votes. Opposing candidates and votes were Green Conley, 76; Tom Witten, 70; and James Waddle, 47.

The old Board of Trustees encountering much opposition was re-elected. Members of the Board and votes received were David Kelley, 181; Wm. (Bill) Fraley, 159; Judge Clifton, 166; M. J. Wells, 176; and Flem Conley, 161.

Opposing candidates and votes received were Wm. Stratton, 141; Cecil Honeycutt, 156; Estill Thacker, 142; Taylor Blair, 140; and John Crum, 154.

The magistrate's race in District No. 2, which includes the town of Van Lear, was also hotly contested. Otis Richmond, Republican, was elected magistrate by a majority of 100 over Roscoe Burton, Democrat, of Van Lear.

One important story that apparently was missed by the local newspaper in 1945 was Consol's merger with Pittsburgh Coal Company. Soon, the combined company, known as Pittsburgh Consolidation Coal Company, began selling off most of its assets in Eastern Kentucky, including the very communities it had created some thirty years earlier.

April 4, 1946—Announcement of the sale of Van Lear, with 2,060 acres of land on Johns Creek, Daniels Creek and Millers Creek in Johnson and Martin counties for $300,000, was made by O. G. Hinton, Pikeville attorney, on Tuesday. It was announced that the sale, which included Van Lear with 247 homes, a clubhouse and an office building, was made by the Pittsburgh-Consolidation Coal Company to Hinton and four associates, John M. Yost, W. Frank Scott, bankers and W. R. Walters, a real estate dealer, all of Pikeville.

It was also disclosed that the plans of the company is to divest itself of its realty holdings in Jenkins and McRoberts in Letcher County. S. M. Cassidy, vice-president of the company, denied that the firm would abandon its Van Lear operation.

"Diamond drilling," he said, "proved that there is sufficient coal for eight to ten years of operation." However, he said, the sale of the realty holding is in line with a new company policy to concentrate on mining and its holding in Letcher County will be sold as soon as the necessary arrangements can be made. The company plans to sell 1,906 houses in Eastern Kentucky to employees on attractive terms. According to the 1940 census the town of Van Lear had a population of 1,723.

Hinton, as spokesman for the group, said that the office building and clubhouse had been leased for two years to the Ryan Construction Company, contractor for the Dewey Reservoir on which work was started recently. The houses in Van Lear will be sold, with the present tenants having the first opportunity to purchase, it was announced by Hinton.

The Consolidation Coal Company merged with the Pittsburgh Coal Company last year, the merger being effective November 23, 1945. This firm is the largest commercial producer of soft coal. The operation at Van Lear began in 1909 and actual output of coal started in 1910. The property was acquired by the Consolidation Coal Company from John C. C. Mayo.

The following summer, Pittsburgh Consolidation Coal announced the creation of a new business entity to oversee the operation of its Kentucky mines.

June 27, 1946—Pittsburgh Consolidation Coal Company announces the formation of "Consolidation Coal Company—Ky."

A wholly-owned subsidiary to take over the operation of its mining properties in the State of Kentucky. These properties consist of Mine 155 at Van Lear, Mine 204 at Jenkins, Mines 206, 206-B and 207 at Dunham, Mine 214 at McRoberts and Clover Splint Mine at Closplint.

Mr. Samuel M. Cassidy has been elected president of the new company with headquarters at Jenkins, Kentucky. Mr. Cassidy is a native Kentuckian. Born in Lexington, his was graduated from the University of Kentucky in 1925 with a degree of mining engineering. He has had a wide experience in coal mining, and prior to coming to Consolidation Coal Company earlier this year; he was managing the coal properties of the Weirton Steel Company in Pennsylvania.

Other newly elected officers of the company are Geo. O. Tarleton, vice-president operations; Madison A. Dunlap, assistant to the president; A. Roy Marlin, manager of properties; Elmer J. Berlin, treas.; Frank H. Price, asst. secretary; and R. J. Howard, chief engineer. Operations will be carried on the same as in the past without change in personnel.

Superintendents of the various operations of the company are Marshall E. Prunty, Mine 204; M. M. McCormick, Mine 155; Wm. A. Stapleton, Mines 206, 206-B and 207; Seth H. Kegan, Mine 214; E. F. Wright, Clover Splint Mine; Steve Barson, Power; Damon

Duncan, Central Shops; Robert Blake, central preparation plant; and Jack McClellan, B & R. Dept.

The formation of a Kentucky company to carry on operations in the State of Kentucky is in line with the company's policy of decentralizing the management of its mining properties in the various states.

The officers of the Ky. Co. are in complete charge of the operations and whether this Kentucky company will be able to grow and become an important factor in Kentucky will depend on these men, and all their fellow employees, as the operations of this company are now entirely separate and independent from those in other states.

In spring 1947, there was a full-page advertisement in the Herald *announcing the sale of forty-nine homes in Van Lear—eleven three-room houses, five four-room houses, and 29 five-room houses with running water and electricity. In the same issue, Pittsburg Consolidation Coal announced the purchase of new equipment it said would extend the life of the Van Lear mine by a decade.*

April 10, 1947—The life of the Pittsburg Consolidation Coal Company Mine 155 at Van Lear, Ky. has been extended as much as ten years as a result of the installation of modern mining equipment and other improvements. Recently, construction work was started on the tipple by Roberts and Schuler Company, Chicago, to install washing and dewatering equipment in an even better grade of the famous Original Millers Creek stoker coal. New types of underground machinery have arrived, including three Joy loaders. Shuttle cars for these loaders will arrive shortly, but in the meantime, loading is being done on shake conveyers.

Work has again started on the Dewey Dam, whose site is located a short distance from Van Lear. Plans are being pushed for the hard surfacing of the gravel road from Van Lear to the dam site.

Despite the merged company's investment in new equipment, Van Lear's heyday was over. Once hailed as "the overnight city," Van Lear's population fell swiftly and sharply, and many of the families that had considered it home soon would receive eviction notices.

May 1, 1947—The auction sale held at Van Lear Saturday by the Walters Realty and Auction Company for the Rice Development Company of Pikeville was stopped after the sale of nine houses was made. Prices of the real estate sold ranged from $800 to $2,300.

The holdings of the Pittsburg-Consolidation Coal Company, including 2,060 acres of land on Johns Creek, Daniels Creek, and Millers Creek, and 247 houses were sold to a group of Pikeville business men in April of last year for $300,000. About 100 of the houses have been sold to Van Lear residents since that time.

Prior to this sale on Saturday, 49 families living in the houses received eviction notices. Many of those receiving these notices have been residents of Van Lear and employees of the Consolidation Coal Company for the past 25 or 30 years. Some had been born and reared in Van Lear.

Among those receiving notices of eviction and who are other older citizens of the town, are Milford Pelphrey, Fred Wetzel, B.F. Sprinkle, Frank Daniel, Frank Campigotto, Dick Blevins, Jarrett Barker, Mrs. E. W. Beers, Mrs. Jim McAllister, Eddie Meade, Murl Meade, Farris Arrowood, Tom Colvin and Green Conley.

Green Conley purchased House No. 129 in which he had resided for the past 24 years. Mr. Conley has been an employee of the Consolidation Coal Company for 38 years, living in Van Lear for the past 35 years. He has reared nine children, seven of whom have graduated from Van Lear High School, and another will graduate this year.

Those who purchased real estate in Saturday's sale are Mrs. James Hayes, Paul Preston, Russell Pack, Wiley Collins, Calvin Webb, John Marshall, Tom Preston, Green Conley and John H. Preston.

In 1940 the town had a population of 1,723, but the population has dropped considerably in the past few years.

Epilogue

Van Lear still exists, but it isn't the same place it was in the first half of the 20th century. Its population peaked at 2,300 in 1930. By the 1960 Census, the number of people who lived at Van Lear had fallen to 900, and most of the town's businesses had closed. In 1963, Van Lear's municipal government was declared inactive by the circuit court.

Van Lear High survived several more years but graduated its last class in 1968; the following year, all of Johnson County's small, rural high schools were consolidated into Johnson Central, in Paintsville.

Van Lear's spirit endures, however. Nearly 2,000 live in the community today, and hundreds more attend the annual town reunion, which is held the first Saturday in August. Most of the major structures built by Consolidation Coal are gone, but the company's Van

Lear office building is now home to the Van Lear Historical Society and Coal Mine Museum.

Index

www.ingramcontent.com/pod-product-compliance
Lightning Source LLC
Chambersburg PA
CBHW051833090426
42736CB00011B/1785